The Tenth Muse

The Tenth Muse

THE PURSUIT OF EARTH SCIENCE

Ronald B. Parker

CHARLES SCRIBNER'S SONS · NEW YORK

Library of Congress Cataloging-in-Publication Data

Parker, Ronald B.
  The tenth muse.

  Includes index.
  1. Earth sciences. I. Title.
QE35.P375 1986   550   86-6581
ISBN 0-684-18608-X

Published simultaneously in Canada
by Collier Macmillan Canada, Inc.

Composition by Maryland Linotype

Manufactured by Fairfield Graphics

Designed by Marek Antoniak

First Edition

Dedicated to my close friend and colleague
Professor Heinrich Toots as a token of
my esteem for his mind and his friendship

Contents

Acknowledgments

Drafts of the essays in this book have been improved in both content and style from critical reading by John King of S.U.N.Y. Buffalo, Heinrich Toots of C. W. Post College, and Mike Voorhies of the University of Nebraska State Museum, and I am grateful to them for their gift of that most precious commodity—time. My wife, Teresa, served, as always, as my official layperson reader and sensible stylist. I also very much appreciate the ideas and directions that have arisen from interchanges with J. R. Beerbower, D. W. Boyd, W. A. Bothner, A. G. Fischer, D. S. Hodge, Sheldon Judson, F. Koenemann, C. E. Mitchell, Marie Morisawa, Jim Sears, and many others. As is customary in such matters, I take full responsibility for any ideas presented here that may be less than conservative and traditional.

"It is precisely for this that I love geology. It is infinite and ill defined: like poetry, it immerses itself in mysteries and floats among them without drowning. It does not manage to lay bare the unknown, but it flaps the surrounding veils to and fro; and every so often gleams of light escape and dazzle one's vision."

—R. Töpffer after being a guest on a field trip with some geologists. From *Nouvelles genevoises* (1841)

The Tenth Muse

Introduction

I have always maintained that geology is the original science. Those who argue that astronomy preceded geology do have a point, and I might even grant them a tie for first if pressed. The nine daughters of Zeus and Mnemosyne were each assigned to be muses to various categories of arts and letters with the last one, Urania, given the responsibility of astronomy. I might even suggest to a protesting astronomer that Urania was really the muse of astrology rather than of the science of the stars, planets, and space; the poet Milton identifies her in *Paradise Lost* as the spirit of the loftiest poetry with no mention of astronomy. Clio, the muse of history, might be a candidate for a muse for geology inasmuch as geology is a highly historical science almost by definition, but because Clio is usually pictured with a scroll and a chest of books, but no geology hammer, I think that might be stretching it.

It is puzzling that the Greeks didn't have a muse for the science of the earth because many of the geological observations of Greek scholars were far closer to the truth than those of so-called scientists who followed millennia later.

Perhaps the Greeks thought that geology could stand on its own merit and required no sponsor in court.

Even so, I propose that a Tenth Muse be created to watch over the science of the whole earth. As to a name, we could look to Anne Bradstreet, author of the first volume of American poetry to be published, in London in 1650. Because of her literary activities Ms. Bradstreet became known as the Tenth Muse. However, Anne showed no interest in earth science as far as I can ascertain, so she seems an improbable candidate to lend her name to muse of the earth sciences. In any case she was daughter of just a governor, not a god. Zeus was a well-known womanizer, and certainly had more than enough daughters to go around, but alas, we have no way of knowing which of them might be suitable.

Perhaps her identity is best left a mystery, like so much about the earth. It is enough to know that there is a Tenth Muse who looks after struggling students mapping, stratigraphers clambering over precipitous slopes to examine a sequence of sedimentary rocks, glaciologists with cold feet, petrologists melting rocks in a laboratory, paleontologists trying to reconstruct past life, and lovers of the earth trying to explain its wonders.

Though we know not her name, we see the presence of the Tenth Muse everywhere there are earth scientists, and even amateurs, for geology is a handy science for amateurs. No fancy equipment is needed to try one's hand at geology. The laboratory is the earth, and many of the experiments need only to be observed to understand them. A careful look is needed, of course, if one is to draw the correct conclusions.

In northern Europe and Britain there are numerous large boulders dotting the landscape in improbable places such as ridge tops and the edge of cliffs. Even more mysterious, the boulders are made of rock types not found in the vicinity. Perhaps under the influence of one of the first nine muses, many people who observed the boulders attributed them to the work of giants who had hurled them about in play or anger. Those literary muses even made their influence felt on a few eighteenth- and nineteenth-century scientists who supposed that the boulders were fired like cannonballs from caves during the uplift of the Alps.

Happily, the observant common man was a better geologist than most of the scientists of the day. The boulders were carried to their present locations by glaciers of the great ice age, but all but a few of the learned men of Europe discounted that idea as nonsense. However, the idea was proposed by a Swiss chamois hunter to a civil engineer and thence to Jean de Charpentier, the manager of a salt mine who was a skilled amateur natural scientist. De Charpentier studied the boulders and other evidence of glaciers for several years, during which field work he discovered that many Swiss peasants had long accepted a glacial theory. He was on the way to a meeting in Lucerne in 1834 to describe his glacial theory, which was to be resoundingly rejected by a distinguished company of scientists, when he stopped to chat with a woodcutter along the road. De Charpentier described the encounter as follows.

> Traveling through the valley of Hasli and Lungern, I met on the Brunig road a woodcutter from Meirungen. We talked and walked together for a while. As I was examining a large boulder of Grimsel granite lying next to the path, he said: "There are many stones of that kind around here, but they come from far away, from the Grimsel, because they consist of Geisberger [granite] and the mountains of this vicinity are not made of it."

> When I asked him how he thought that these stones had reached their location, he answered without hesitation: "The Grimsel glacier transported them on both sides of the valley, because that glacier extended in the past as far as the town of Bern, indeed water could not have deposited them at such an elevation above the valley bottom, without filling the lakes."

In a more modern case, I visited a graduate student in his field area to help him with any problems he might have encountered. We looked at one hill that was set off from the main mass of the Medicine Bow Mountains in Wyoming. After looking at the orientation of structures in the rocks, I mentioned that it looked to me as if the whole mass had become detached and rotated as it moved downhill to its present location, because the structures were oriented quite differently. The graduate student looked at me suspiciously and asked if I was pulling his leg. I told him that I was quite serious. He then smiled and said that the reason he asked is that an old hermit who lived in the area, Pop Worth, had told him that the hill in question was "upside down." Pop was quite correct as it turned out. The student, Jack King, now a professor at S.U.N.Y. Buffalo, wrote a paper about the occurrence and received lots of flak from a number of professional geologists who didn't believe what the hermit, Jack, and I had perceived clearly.

This is not to say that every Swiss woodcutter and Wyoming hermit is a skilled geologist, but the evidence is all around us for anyone to look at, and the interpretation of unsophisticated observers may be just as reasonable as that of a highly trained specialist. In some ways, a layperson is better equipped to see a relationship among geologic features, because he or she doesn't carry the intellectual prejudices that a professional does. Many early so-called scientists were so concerned with trying to fit observations into a religiously defined model that they came to ridiculous conclusions. Their training in religion and the arts was a serious disadvantage to them.

Although I think an open, unfettered mind has many advantages, I've assumed that readers of this volume have already read my *Inscrutable Earth* or are somewhat familiar with some elementary geologic concepts. The essays can be read in any order, although they are arranged in such a way as to present some concepts in a logical manner. Thus it is useful to know what a "hot spot" is as described in "When

Vulcan Speaks" when I propose an explanation for the arrangement of Iranian salt domes in "Salt Rising." "The View from Olympus" likewise provides background for a fuller appreciation of "Elysian Fields."

I placed "The Buffer Did It" in the number-one slot because the buffer paradigm has almost completely general application in the sciences of the earth. It encompasses phenomena as disparate as a tiny geyser at Yellowstone and the breakup of supercontinents and plate tectonics. The buffer concept as discussed here is the most up to date in print, even in the professional journals. I would hope that some amateur geologists might spot the work of buffers in some of their own observations. After all, buffers are the things that make the earth work the way it does. Perhaps the buffer paradigm is a gift of that same mysterious Tenth Muse who looked over the shoulders of that Swiss woodcutter and old Pop Worth.

CHAPTER ONE

The Buffer Did It

My colleague Heinrich Toots and I were driving through the Minnesota countryside in the summer of 1983—talking geology. We explored a number of topics including the manner in which sedimentary rocks become deposited. Various earth scientists had various concepts, and neither Toots or I agreed with any of them entirely. Like all scientists we were searching for generalities that would help our understanding of the process. There was the generality that water moves downhill, and may carry sediment with it in the process, but did that concept have value beyond the obvious? Suddenly I realized that the whole process was one of energy storage and release. The water and the loose sediment moved because it could move to a state of lower energy. The water and sediment could accumulate at a relatively high energy state at some level, then move to a lower level with a lower energy state—following that fundamental law of nature that spontaneous reactions go in the direction of lowering of total energy. I told Toots "I've got it, it's energy storage." I don't remember saying "aha!" or "eureka!", though Toots thinks I might have. He and I realized that the idea was a generalization about geologic processes that had wide application, far wider than just transport and deposition of sediments. Toots told me I was on to something important, and I happily agreed. Neither of us realized at the time how important the energy storage concept would become.

Science often works just the way it worked that Minnesota summer morning. The rough outline of a theory appears in someone's mind—very often in the course of a discussion with a colleague or while trying to explain something to a student or lay person. Ideas don't usually appear fully formed, but a basic framework leaps to mind, a framework that can be built upon if the concept proves to be useful.

Thomas Edison is credited with saying something to the extent that genius is 1 percent inspiration and 99 percent perspiration. That may well have been true for Edison, and perhaps for other inventors of gadgets who, like Edison, have only an elementary or even incorrect grasp of theory, but are clever with trial and error experimentation. Lots of technological advances are the 99 percent sweat variety, but science rarely works that way.

One might paraphrase Edison for science by saying that scientific theories are all inspiration, but the inspiration is followed by endless testing. Testing of ideas *is* the scientific method. Testing of a theory takes place over and over again, and it is inherent in science that nothing is ever really proved, but valid generalizations that survive repeated testing become entrenched in the working kit of science. When a major idea fails to meet testing, it is discarded and a new theory must rise to fill its place.

But, back to the story. I, like so many earth scientists of my generation, was raised on a solid, conservative, and substantial diet of gradualism. Gradualism is a concept championed by the great nineteenth century English geologist Charles Lyell, who called it uniformitarianism. Gradualism imagines that geologic processes take place in tiny increments of geologic work that are integrated together to result in mountain building, erosion of mountains to stubs, and transport of sediment to quiet depositional sites.

Realists didn't really accept the gradualist framework entirely, and Lyell himself softened his stance later in his career, because it is obvious to anyone that geologic processes are seldom gradual. Instead, we observe isolated volcanic eruptions, dumping of ice-dammed lakes, earthquakes, surging glaciers, cyclic and periodic deposition of sediment, and so forth.

In an attempt to bring concept in line with actuality, earth scientists in various disciplines altered their views of earth processes and tried to fit what they observed into a system that assumed a complex group of equilibrium processes that were related to one another by exchanges of energy and by movement of matter from one equilibrium system to another. Proponents spoke of a dynamic earth and an engine earth, terms that expressed belief in a family of processes driven by energy from various internal and external sources. The concept of dynamic equilibrium was espoused many years ago by Grove Karl Gilbert, a mathematically inclined geologist with the U.S. Geological Survey (USGS). He suggested his ideas in a classic paper on the geology of the Henry Mountains in Utah published in 1877 and followed up with other works, including a monograph on the transportation of sediment by water in 1914. Gilbert brought a quantification to sedimentary geology and to geomorphology, the study of landforms, that brought to those fields the sort of thinking that had already pervaded the so-called hard-rock fields of petrology and geochemistry. Gilbert's concepts were very influential and, until just a few years ago, the belief in equilibrium among different parts of a geologic system was accepted without question.

In a 1980 paper, geomorphologists Don Coates of SUNY Binghamton and John Vitek of Oklahoma State described the status of quantitative geomorphology in the 1960s and 1970s as follows:

> Thus the common denominator of such work has been recognition of factors related to the stability of systems. The goals of such studies were the establishment of criteria, arguments, and equations that identified a balanced and harmonious landscape.
>
> The element that has been missing from these paradigms is the failure to analyze the other side of the coin—how to identify, describe, and measure an unbalanced system or one that is on the verge of becoming disharmonious.

That quote may seem like an erudite way of saying a very simple thing, but we should always remember that important ideas are frequently simple ones. The late Marshall Kay of Columbia University once told a lecture audience on Long Island that every time he had gotten an original and powerful idea, his immediate reaction was 'How could I have been so stupid as to have not seen that before?"

Geomorphologist and sedimentationist Stan Schumm of Colorado State University introduced a concept of thresholds to his field in 1973. Schumm's thresholds were points at which geologic change were thought to take place. A threshold is crossed when a mass of rock waste and soil on a slope suddenly moves downhill as a landslide, mudflow, or rock fall. A threshold is crossed when the transporting power of a stream is increased and the mode of motion of bottom sediment changes.

The threshold idea caught on with the geomorphic community and brought those workers more into line with other earth scientists who had used the concept under different names for a much longer time; for example, when a rock fails by faulting, melts, or is metamorphosed, a threshold has been crossed .

However, according to my energy storage concept, real geologic events are more than just a collection of thresholds. In the budget of geologic events there are inputs of energy that are expended to do geologic work. The input of energy may be by many means, although the ultimate source for all geologic work is internal heat from the earth and solar radiation. That energy can be expended or stored in some form. Stored energy can be released to produce abrupt geologic events and the change in energy from one form to another provides a timing mechanism for events, as well. Most geologic events are probably controlled by rates of processes rather than by equilibrium relations, even dynamic equilibrium. The equilibrium concept is a handy one to lean upon—partly because the mathematics of equilibrium processes is simpler than that for rate-controlled ones—but in the real world most events are one-way events that proceed spontaneously. The equilibrium concept requires that processes in the earth be at a delicate balance at all times, whereas I have the view that earth systems are in a state of unbalance—disequilibrium— with one another. I have called my energy storage idea the buffer paradigm or buffer hypothesis. The buffer paradigm provides a conceptual framework for a great majority— perhaps all—geologic events.

I will describe my buffer paradigm in its current form and will also delve into the process of how a scientist disseminates a new idea to colleagues—how it works and how it doesn't work. I'll relate my own experience to illustrate the functioning of a body of individuals who are tied together by many common interests, yet who are mostly specialists in one or more limited disciplines.

As I said at the beginning, I assumed that the storage of energy and its subsequent release must be important. In the case of sediments being deposited in a depositional basin, I had proposed to Toots that the sediment accumulated in a sort of temporary storage area until the mass became unstable, at which point erosion and transportation to a final depositional site would take place. In such a system the final sedimentary sequence would be a cyclic or repetitive one, with each unit accumulating during a relatively short interval of mobilization of stored sediment. That episode would be followed by an interval of nondeposition in the main basin while new sediment accumulated in the temporary storage area. The situation can be compared with accumulation of snow—an airborne sediment—on a roof. The snow pack builds up until it becomes unstable or until a thaw triggers instability. At that point the snow slides off of the roof to a new site, and the process starts over again. Through the course of the winter the sequence might be repeated many times—to the annoyance of whoever shovels the snow. The snow which accumulates from the slides off the roof is deposited during brief events even though the accumulation on the roof could be more or less continuous or related to periodic weather events. Because the stored sediment was at a higher potential energy location than the final resting place, I called the concept energy storage. For the entity where energy was stored, I proposed the term buffer.

I use the term buffer in a way similar to its use in computer jargon; that is, a buffer is a place of temporary storage. I quickly realized that many geologic systems can be placed in the framework of energy storage in buffers. I thought about the concept through the course of a year and fine-tuned some of the ideas, then submitted a short article on the subject to the journal *Geology*.

Meanwhile, I took the show on the road. I wrote a number of colleagues in the Northeast and set up a schedule of lectures at a number of universities. Some of the lectures were aimed at the general public, but most were to small groups of faculty and graduate students. The lectures gave me the chance to get a lot of feedback in a short time. Such lectures are also useful in that the audience generally contains a broad spectrum of specialists in many fields, and I wanted to bounce the concept off people outside my principal areas of competence. Over the course of the year I lectured at a dozen campuses. Each lecture brought new and different responses. I was greeted with enthusiasm, indifference, outrage, puzzlement, you name it.

My first talk was at C. W. Post College on Long Island, my colleague Toots' home base. The audience there was a mixture of geologists and the general public. The ideas got a warm reception. An economist came up to me after one talk and said that he thought the concept would be very powerful in his discipline!

The next day I spoke at Princeton, and was pleased to hear that my host, geomorphologist Sheldon Judson, thought my concept gave him a useful framework for putting together some work on streams that he had done in Italy, and that he had not yet been able to describe.

At my next stop, SUNY Binghamton, the students were strangely silent during the question period following my talk. The department head, Dick Beerbower, who had been a reviewer of my *Geology* paper, confided to me that he thought the students were so used to hearing about minutiae that they didn't quite know what to do with a broad, philosophical talk like mine. Afterward at an informal social gathering, I heard the words energy storage and buffer tossed back and forth by the same students, so the idea was generating interest, after all—it just took a while to sink in.

I followed up that stop with one at the University of New Hampshire and then SUNY Buffalo. At New Hampshire I gathered more comments, including some powerful insights from a graduate student, Falk Koenemann. I had fine-tuned my talk throughout the trip as I had opportunities to exchange ideas with more and more scientists, and was probably at my best at the last stop, Buffalo, where the audience response was also the most positive.

My paper was accepted and published, and I continued to set up lectures. My experience with trying to introduce a new idea is far from unique, though the details of any given sequence would be different. There are those who resist any new idea, those who embrace almost any new idea, those who think the new idea isn't new at all, and every other variation. The scientist who believes in an idea pursues peers through talks and in the published literature. Many good ideas die for lack of support, many are shown to be inadequate or even just plain incorrect, and others just get lost when their originator gets fed up with trying to push them. Some ideas fail to persuade the scientific community because at the time some critical bit of evidence was lacking, and the whole theory was set aside until a key bit of information showed up. I'm happy to report that the buffer concept is progressing well as far as I can tell. It used to be easier to judge the reception of a published paper by the number of requests one received for reprints of the work. In these days of ubiquitous photocopiers, such requests are comparatively rare, but I've received more than enough to be flattered.

I'll summarize some major aspects of the buffer paradigm as it now stands. New applications and properties seem to appear almost daily, but here's the present version. Geologic buffers are entities that can store or expend energy. In some instances stored energy is available to do geologic work such as sediment transport or shaking down of mountain sides. In others, a buffer just acts as a timer, setting the length of an interval during which a process takes place. The buffer idea supposes that most geologic systems are out of balance with their environment—at a potentially unstable high energy state. Sort of like a teenaged boy behind the wheel of a car—an event waiting to happen.

Buffers have a number of properties. They have a maximum storage capacity. Capacity might be the amount of heat that can be stored in a geyser or a volcano, the amount of elastic strain that can be stored in a piece of the earth's crust, the volume of water stored behind a natural dam, the buoyant gravitative energy stored in a buried salt mass, or the potential energy in a mass of volcanic ash or other loose material on a hillside.

Buffers aren't all perfect storage units, either. One that contains all the energy put into it can be said to be a competent buffer. Most real buffers are less than perfect, and they generally leak. The capacity of a buffer can be limited by its leak rate. For example, if a body of water formed behind a dam produced by a rockfall into a canyon, there would be a certain amount of water that would leak through the dam or into permeable rock layers in the canyon bottom and walls. The higher the water rose behind the dam, the higher the pressure would be at the leaky places, and the greater would be the leak rate. Thus, the capacity of the lake might be limited by the point at which it rose high enough for leaks to equal inputs, even though that might be reached at a level below the top of the dam. The dam could be compared to a tire with a slow leak. The more air one pumps into the tire, the faster the leak becomes until at a certain air pressure no amount of pumping will keep up with the leak.

There are analogous leaks in other buffer systems. Some volcanoes rarely or never produce large eruptions because gases and lava are frequently emitted in small amounts. Some blocks of the crust never store enough elastic energy for release as an earthquake because the energy is slowly released by movement on small faults or slippage along internal layering of some sort.

Some buffers are totally leaky and one might be tempted to argue that if a buffer is completely incompetent to store energy in some form then there is no buffer at all. That is not a useful way to treat that condition though, because such a buffer can serve as a timing buffer, even if there is no energy storage. I'll come back to this point.

Buffers can release their stored energy in response to external events or when some internal stabilizing barrier—a threshold—is exceeded. Transport of sediment stored in a buffer such as a mass along a stream margin or on the slope of a marine basin can be triggered by a heavy rainfall or by an earthquake. The sediment buffer can then be said to be entrained in the triggering phenomenon, which may itself be the product of some other buffer emptying. Many buffers presumably persist in a metastable state for long intervals prior to emptying through triggering by external or internal influences.

Energy stored in a buffer can be stored in many forms. Some of the stored energy is quickly available to do geologic work such as stored water, elastic strain, or gas pressure. Other energy may be stored in forms that are not quickly convertible and as such do little geologic work. Energy is stored in crystallization of new minerals in a rock mass subjected to higher temperatures. That energy is as real as storage of heat in the form of temperature increase, but unlike such heat, the heat stored in the new, metamorphic minerals can be released only very slowly by processes of physical and chemical weathering.

Depending on their properties, buffers can act as active participants in geologic events, not only setting the timing but releasing the energy that causes a given event—or they can play a mediating role, influencing the course and timing of events but not really participating in the sense of contributing energy to a process in an obvious way.

Buffers that store energy frequently release that energy in abrupt, even catastrophic, events. The phenomenon is well illustrated by the behavior of geysers. With a geyser, energy is stored in a mass of water in the form of heat. Many scientists studied the *Geysir* in Iceland, which gave its name to all such spouters, and various theories were proposed. The most widely accepted one was that of Bunsen (of Bunsen burner fame), who proposed that the phenomenon was caused by heating of water to a temperature above the boiling point from which it was able to flash to a boil with eruption of the column of water. Bunsen devised a metal model of his theoretical geyser that was copied and used to dampen the lecture stand of many a professor. In spite of the popularity of the Bunsen geyser as a teaching aid, detractors argued—and rightly so—that Bunsen's model was too simple and didn't really explain all geysers, but as with many phenomena, interest in geysers waned as geologists went off in different scholarly directions, and they are barely mentioned today, even in elementary textbooks.

According to the simple, Bunsen-type model, the timing

of eruptions is a function of the rate of heat flow to the water buffer, and the volume of the buffer. The faster the rate of heat flow and the smaller the buffer, the shorter the interval to fill the buffer and the shorter the interval between eruptions. If that was literally the case, then geysers would all be more faithful than Old Faithful, and they're not. Also, according to Bunsen's ideas, a geyser should reach a critical level of instability, erupt in one great blast, then start the cycle again. Real geysers, or at least most of them, don't do that.

I had discussed the release of energy by geysers with Toots, and concluded that the release wasn't all at once, but in a series of steps leading up to the main eruption. I termed such a sequence the *geyser effect*, and he and I discussed a number of examples of such a stepwise energy release.

Although I had visited Yellowstone Park a number of times I had never before noted the step-by-step anatomy of a geyser eruption, so I went there to see how my predicted geyser effect really worked—to test my theory. I knew in advance that geysers weren't as regular as Bunsen's theory would have us believe. For example, Old Faithful, the archetypal regular geyser averages about 64 minutes between eruptions, but intervals range from extremes of 33 and 148 minutes. I also knew from previous visits that the eruption of Old Faithful was not in one big burst, but I had never paid attention to the details. I found that there are many, small preeruptions during which the water just swells up from the orifice a bit or small fountains a few feet high rise up. The preeruptive activity takes place over a period of 10 or 15 minutes or more, with the eruptions gradually increasing in height and the interval between successive eruptions diminishing in a most irregular way. The main eruption sequence is also not a single eruption; rather, individual pulses become stronger and closer together until finally they almost blend to produce a continuous major eruption that lasts for as long as 5 minutes, after which it decays in steps to relative inactivity. When I

visited Old Faithful I found that it was very easy to study
the eruption sequence. With each little preeruption, the
assembled crowd of tourists would gasp expectantly and
chatter to one another, then give a group sigh of disap-
pointment when the hoped-for big blast failed to materialize.
If one wanted to study the eruption sequence over a long
time period, all that would be needed is a microphone and
a tape recorder stashed under a bench in the observation
area and a computer with sound recognition capabilities to
listen to the tape and note the timing of the aws! of dis-
appointment, the oohs! of anticipation and excitement, and
the aahs! of satisfaction and wonder at the full eruption.

But back to energy release. The geyser effect is a sequence
whereby energy release takes place over an extended period
of time with many small releases which build in an exponential fashion to a final group of events of large magnitude. I found on my pilgrimage to Yellowstone that the
geyser effect is also well illustrated by a smaller geyser in
the Upper Basin of Yellowstone Park—just down the road
from Old Faithful—called Rusty Geyser. Trusty Rusty
erupts every one to three minutes according to former Yellowstone Park Naturalist T. Scott Bryan, though when I
observed it in 1985, it erupted repeatedly on a two-and-a-
half-minute period. I assume that there is seasonal and other
long-term variation, but for any given period of time it gives
the geyser watcher lots of looks at the geyser effect. Rusty
doesn't attract a big crowd of fans like Old Faithful, but
it gives a dandy show for buffs—a name coined for adherents of the buffer paradigm by Sheldon Judson.

To clarify why there is a geyser effect with energy release
from natural geysers, we can move our attention to a man-
made geyser north of Lakeview in the south-central part of
Oregon. The Lakeview geyser is an uncapped, drilled well
in the middle of a shallow pond. It not only erupts with
great regularity, but its eruptions are not full geyser-effect
eruptions, because there are no preeruptions. The geyser
just starts squirting out a column of water that rapidly

increases in height, then decays. What we see at the Lakeview geyser is a very simple buffer, not unlike Professor
Bunsen's metal demonstration model, for it is just a cylindri-
cal body of water in a smooth tube. The water reaches the
boiling point, boils to empty the tube, and that's it. The
exponential final release of water is displayed but the
gradual, pulsing buildup is absent.

Real geysers consist of more complicated plumbing, with
twists and ends and places for steam to accumulate and
many connected chambers and passageways. The usual
geyser eruption is the release of many chambers—buffers—
together in a complicated interaction, so we observe not a
simple, one-shot release but a complex event.

Other buffer-produced events show the geyser effect as
well. The release of water from ice-dammed lakes follows
an exponential increase in flow rate after preliminary minor
outpourings. The surging of surge glaciers is preceded by
the "minisurges" first observed by Barclay Kamb and his
co-workers, which are followed by a rapid increase in rate
of movement. Great volcanic eruptions are heralded by all
manner of activity from the seismic to the eruptive. The list
is endless. Emptying of natural buffers appears to produce
a predictable sequence of events.

The geyser effect is seemingly so universal that it also
provides a way of determining whether or not a buffering
phenomenon is operating. The buffers are obvious in the
foregoing examples, but we can also detect geyser-effect
phenomena in other events that suggest a buffer at work.
The case of extinctions of organisms is an interesting one.
As mentioned in this volume, the extinctions at the end of
the Pleistocene epoch may well have been a part of a decline of mammals in general, or may have been caused
catastrophically by some external event. In other words was
the cause internal to a buffer, or was it caused by some
other process?

That same sort of question can be asked about the great
extinction at the end of the Cretaceous Period, in which the

dinosaurs and much of the marine life of the time died and
which some attribute to the effect of impact of an extraterrestrial body. If that sort of "instant" event was the cause,
then there should be no geyser effect whatsoever, because
the event would have been sudden and unheralded. In fact,
it appears that such is not the case. The abrupt extinction
of certain groupings of animals is pointed to by the im-
pacters as evidence of a sudden, brutal event. The impact
hypothesis has, ironically, sent many geologists and paleontologists back to the rocks to go over the fossiliferous strata
inch by inch, as well as back to the books to look at the
whole picture. The evidence emerging now is that the extinctions were, in the first place, far from total at the end
of the Cretaceous Period. Paleontologist Keith Rigby, Jr.,
of Notre Dame has even found a new form of dinosaur
appearing in the very earliest part of the Paleocene Epoch,
after the supposed total wipeout of the giant reptiles. Moreover, the great extinction seems to be simply the culmina-
tion of a long series of extinction events. As University of
Colorado paleontologist Erle Kauffman jokingly commented
during a recent talk at the University of Nebraska—one
wonders how the organisms knew the impacting object was
coming. It appears that the great extinction is the peak of
a geyser-effect phenomenon, and where there is a geyser
effect, there is a buffer. It is now a matter of discerning
what the buffer or system of buffers consists of.

As I have mentioned, some buffers don't store energy at
all and hence play no role in causing catastrophic release of
energy. Buffers can, however, play the role of timers and
control the tempo of events. With the permanent deformation of rocks by folding, faulting, and other means there
may well be little or no energy stored, but the rocks under-
going deformation act as an energy sink, and the rates of
possible deformation determine the length of a period of
mountain building, basin sinking, or other related events.
In an even simpler case, the rate of rebound of a mass of
depressed crust is determined by the rate of adjustment of

the underlying mantle in response to buoyant rising of low-density crust. Such crustal rise may even take place in a series of rapid jumps, producing the appearance of periodic mountain-building or basin-lowering events such as some would attribute to large-scale external forces.

The rate of propagation of fractures can constitute a timing buffer. I had this concept brought home when a baseball-sized hailstone cracked the windshield of my car. The original crack slowly lengthened over the course of the next couple of months. I made the playful assumption that the windshield was a scale model of the continental crust, and calculated how long it would take for a crack to propagate across North America. The result was thirty million years. Great events of earth history commonly involve the formation of rift valleys or the splitting of a block of crust. Observations on the rate of propagation of the East Pacific Rise, a boundary between two oceanic plates, indicate that it has grown at the rate of about 2,000 kilometers (1,200 miles) per ten million years. Given a block of crust of known size, we can use that figure as an approximation for how long it would take to split it apart. In other words, if the North American plate were to split along an east west line during some event, it would take about twenty-five to thirty million years—my car's windshield wasn't such a bad model. In such an event, the buffer just expends energy required to propagate the fracture, none is stored, but the timer effect works all the same.

It has been suggested that continental crust is weaker than oceanic and, further, that thick crust is weaker than thin crust. Expanding on that idea, A. F. Glazner and J. M. Bartley of the University of North Carolina have recently calculated models of thickening of continental crust by the process of piling slices of crust on top of one another— what a structural geologist calls thrust faulting. They propose that the thickened crust would be weakened by accumulation of heat from the decay of radioactive elements and that with normal sorts of rates of erosion from the mass, the minimum strength would be reached in thirty to thirty-five million years.

I propose that buffers control the timing of the formation and breakup of supercontinents by mechanisms such as those just mentioned. The classic case of junction and subsequent breakup was proposed by Canadian geophysicist J. Tuzo Wilson. According to his scenario, now called the Wilson Cycle, there was an ocean in about the present site of the North Atlantic from late Precambrian until about Middle Ordovician time. Then from the Middle Ordovician until the end of the Carboniferous Period the ocean was absent, with the continents of North America and Europe joined. During Permian, Triassic, and Jurassic time there was no deep ocean, and starting at the beginning of the Cretaceous Period, the Atlantic has been opening until this day. The Wilson Cycle would seem to be explainable by a buffer model in much the style of Glazner and Bartley. Continental joining would result in initial strengthening, but gradual weakening would occur from buildup of heat from the earth's interior and from radioactive elements in the mountains formed at the juncture of the masses. Fracture propagation would begin at one or more points to form the precursor of the mid-Atlantic ridge. Inasmuch as the present ridge stretches from off the tip of South America to north of Greenland, a distance of about seventeen thousand kilometers we could imagine that fracture propagation might take eighty-five million years. That assumes that the fracture started at one end and propagated to the other—perhaps not terribly reasonable, except that the East Pacific Rise seems to have done that.

According to Wilson's model, the continents were continuous with one another for about 185 million years. An approximate time budget might be as follows: for the two masses colliding and forming a mountainous junction like the Alpine-Himalayan chain, we could assume that the rate of closure was about the same as the rate of formation of the Alpine-Himalayan chain, or roughly the time since the end of the Cretaceous Period—65 million years. Then, about 35 million years for the buffer of thick crust to weaken, and 85 million years or less for fracture propagation to form the precursor to the mid-Atlantic Ridge. These are very approximate estimates, but they just happen to add up to 185 million years.

As of now, I'm still preaching the buffer story, trying to generate new buffs, and discovering applications in almost every corner of the earth sciences. Buffers are so much a part of the scene that they are as easy to overlook as the butler in the old detective stories. He was never suspected because he was such a familiar part of the household and always seemed so loyal to the family. Buffers are just the same. They're right there under our noses, and they're nearly always a part of the geologic event. We can learn from those old novels—the buffer did it.

CHAPTER TWO

The Urge to Surge

Most people in temperate climes have never seen a glacier, but still they have some impression of what a glacier is and how it behaves. Naturally everyone knows that they are made of ice and are therefore cold. Even the word glacial is used to mean frigid or cold when applied to a person. Glacial also indicates slowness in reference to the supposed, almost imperceptible movement of a glacier. Glacial can carry the sense of unsympathetic, I suppose, because of the idea that a glacier moves inexorably onward, crushing everything in its path.

All of those meanings of the English word glacial have a measure of geologic reality associated with them. Glaciers are cold. A glacier is at the freezing point or below, although a person on its surface may be comfortable in a pair of shorts and no shirt on a sunny summer day—provided he or she wears warm socks and boots. The slowness of glaciers is somewhat exaggerated. To be sure, many glaciers appear not to move at all, and a person on the great ice cap of Greenland or Antarctica would be hard pressed to detect movement without sensitive instruments. Many glaciers, however, move at a fair clip. Valley glaciers move at about

10 to 200 meters (35 to 650 feet) per year. Large glaciers that come off of the Antarctic ice sheet move at 300 to 1,400 meters (1,000 to 4,500 feet) per year, and the Jakobshavn glacier, one of the large ones in Greenland, moves 10 kilometers (6 miles) a year at its end in the sea.

Such are not speeds that threaten to overtake the unwary traveler, but they are far from stationary. For real speed we must turn to the racers of the glacier world, the surge glaciers. These travelers in the fast lane of the glacier clan move at rates of several kilometers in a matter of a few months. Kutiah Glacier in the Karakorams of North Kashmir advanced 12 kilometers (7 miles) in three months in 1953, which is about as fast as the tip of the second hand on a wristwatch. Not exactly screaming down the valley, but I wouldn't want to set up camp on top of it.

I'll come back to surge glaciers, but first a look at glaciers in general will be useful. Glaciers form when snow accumulations fail to melt away during the warm season. Accumulated snow gradually packs down into ice as the snow changes from an air-filled mass to pellets of ice to solid ice by a process of compaction, melting, and refreezing. Glacier ice is not pure ice, for it contains trapped air bubbles from the original snow. The bubbles are confined under pressure, because trapped air cannot escape as the granular snow mass compacts and solidifies into ice. A visitor to a glacier can verify this fact by putting some glacial ice in a glass of water. As the ice warms and melts, the bubbles pop with considerable violence. I spent a year in Greenland while in the army, and no drink was considered properly made if the ice didn't crackle and pop. Glacial ice usually also contains some sediment, and a mustache to filter out the sand from that last drop of whiskey and water was considered de rigueur in the Transportation Arctic Group.

Ice is a solid, but it is able to deform plastically, that is, without breaking, under natural conditions, especially when it is near the melting point. Ice deforms in two ways. One of these is similar to the ductile behavior of metals. Just as a penny placed on a railroad track gets flattened to a thin disk by a passing train, so does a pile of ice like the Greenland ice cap flatten slowly from its own weight. Glaciers flow off the ice cap down valleys just as glaciers in mountainous regions flow down valleys under the pull of gravity.

Ice also deforms by a process of melting and refreezing. Ice is one of the unusual solids that takes up more volume per unit weight as a solid than it does as a liquid, a property it shares with waxes such as paraffin and with printer's type metal, which expands to fill its mold tightly when cast. Because ice is less dense than water, compressing it causes it to melt. This behavior explains the almost frictionless glide of an ice skater, for the runners ride on a film of water generated by the pressure of the weight of the skater—a film that promptly refreezes after the skater has passed. Compaction of ice granules into solid ice is a result of the melting-freezing phenomenon. The weight of the overlying mass is supported at points where adjacent ice granules are in contact. Therefore, the pressure is high at those points, so melting takes place. The water formed moves a short distance and freezes. Thus, contact points shrink as voids become filled with ice. The same sort of thing happens within and around the glacier, especially at the base. As the glacier moves slowly down a valley, it rubs against protuberances in the underlying rock. Where the ice presses against a barrier, the pressure increase can cause melting. The water formed moves to the other side of the object to refreeze in the relatively lower pressure environment.

Thus, by some combination of those two modes, a glacier is able to move as a solid mass. All of the behavior of ice is not plastic, however. Ice can also behave in a brittle manner. So it is that the surface of glaciers is often cut by deep cracks called crevasses. Crevasses are not bottomless pits but are limited to about 25 meters (80 feet) deep; below that depth the ice closes gaps by plastic flow. Crevasses are lovely places provided one doesn't fall into them accidentally. They are generally not open all the way to the bottom, because there are snow and ice bridges across them at intervals. The bridges form at the surface each warm season and move downward relative to the surface as new snow is added to the top. If one breaks through all the bridges to the real bottom of the crevasse, there is commonly water flowing along the base of the crack. Also, the walls, sides, and floor are decorated with giant icicles in the warm season and huge platelike ice crystals in the cold times, the whole illuminated by a lovely soft blue light transmitted through the ice and snow.

The water flowing along crevasses is one aspect of glaciers that is not obvious from the top. Most glaciers are not solid ice except during very cold periods, and most have more or less water under and within the body of ice. Much of the movement of glaciers is by sliding on a layer of water under the mass. There is much disagreement on the amount of water under a glacier, but all agree that it is there. With many glaciers, water flows from the terminus, at least seasonally. The water flowing from a glacier is generally milky looking, for it is filled with suspended sediment from the grinding action of the glacier over its bed. Coarser debris is also carried along with the milky water or accumulates on the surface and in front of the glacier. Concentrations of coarse debris form the streaks called moraines.

The source of water in glaciers is internal, from melting by pressure, from melting of the surface during warm seasons, from rainfall, and from streams that may enter the glacial valley. Water seldom reaches the surface, since the density of the ice is less than water, with the result that the glacier would float if the water was deeper than about 90 percent of the depth of the ice. In most instances, floating would actually be impossible, since the volume of the water is so much smaller than the volume of the ice, but a buoyant and lubricating effect is produced in watery glaciers that enhances movement by slip along the base. With many glaciers, slip along the base is a major mechanism of the overall downslope movement.

Thus we can visualize glaciers as masses of ice that can move by plastic deformation as well as slip along the base, provided the base isn't frozen down. Near the surface and along the edges the ice may behave in a brittle manner, forming crevasses and other features. This mode is satisfactory for explaining most glacier behavior but fails for surge glaciers.

With surge glaciers, movement is not at all the stately and inexorable kind. Surge glaciers remain pretty much stable for many years, then suddenly move. It is just this behavior that makes them hard to study, and the surge phenomenon is one of the major unknowns of glaciology. In addition, since surge glaciers are located in remote regions, usually the surging is not discovered until after it has already happened—too late for many meaningful observations. Measurements must be made for many years prior to the surge, and scientists are reluctant to invest the time and effort to make studies of a glacier that might not surge at all. It is a bit hard to explain to a granting agency that the $250,000 you spent measuring XYZ Glacier has so far produced no results because it hasn't surged yet, but you would like another $300,000 just in case it surges in the next few years.

One person, Austin Post of the University of Washington, has spent a lifetime flying over mountains and glaciers, making observations and taking photographs. He observed over twenty surge glaciers in Alaska and adjacent Canada during a five-year period in the early 1960s. He observed one glacier, Muldrow Glacier in Alaska, prior to and just after a surge episode in the winter of 1956–57. He found that the upper reaches of the glacier were unaffected, but below a break in slope from the high mountain parts to the lower gradient valley there was substantial motion. The movement resulted in a thinning of the glacier in the upper half and a thickening in the lower half resulting from a movement of about 6.5 kilometers (4 miles) in not more than the nine months since he had last observed Muldrow. Similar observations have been made by others. Some have noted a fracture between the uppermost, unaffected part and the surging part, indicating that the surging part pulled away independent of the remainder.

Ordinary glaciers have moraines exposed in long lines parallel to the valley walls. In surge glaciers the moraines form loops spaced at intervals down the valley. Each loop is thought to represent a surge, and the regular succession of loops is indicative of periodic surging. The interval between surges is thought to be roughly constant for a given glacier, with intervals typically in the range of ten to one hundred years.

Surge glaciers also have stagnant regions near the terminus, and the surging does not actually advance the bottom end of the glacier at all, but just redistributes ice within the glacier. They also tend to be relatively long.

The surge phenomenon was first observed at Variegated Glacier, Alaska, in 1906. Since then, according to Austin Post, Variegated has surged in the late 1920s or early 1930s, in about 1947, and in 1964–65. With a recurrence period of about seventeen to twenty years, a surge was expected in the years 1981–85. Barclay Kamb of Cal Tech, C. F. Raymond of the University of Washington, and others began studying Variegated Glacier in 1973 in anticipation of a surge. They found that the ice was thickening in the upper part of the glacier and thinning in the lower part. In addition to the change in thickness, the normal slow movement of the glacier increased over the interval from 1973 to 1981. Also, until 1978 the flow increase was more marked during summer than winter, indicating more basal sliding in summer. Starting in 1978, the flow increase continued in winter. Beginning in 1978 and continuing through 1981, the team noticed brief periods of rapid movement during summer that they dubbed minisurges. During a minisurge the flow velocity increased over an hour or two to up to almost ten times the normal movement, then slowed down over ten to twenty hours to return to the normal speed. During minisurges water rose in boreholes in the glacier to heights above the base of up to 90 percent of the thickness of the ice at the borehole. Because of that observation the team attributed the rapid movement to high water pressure under the glacier that permitted rapid basal sliding.

The real surging began in January 1982 when the rate of flow slowly increased over several months to a value several times normal. In late May the movement underwent rapid acceleration to a peak in late June, after which speeds decayed back to almost normal levels. An increase began again in October, and ice-movement velocities gradually increased to a peak in January 1983, with a decay, then another climb to the most rapid movement of the surge in June 1983, when the glacier moved at peak speeds of 14 meters (45 feet) per day. Movement then slowed down to normal values by mid-July.

Kamb, Raymond, and their colleagues attributed the rapid movement to an increase in water pressure under the glacier that lubricated the base and lifted it free of objects on the rock bottom. Part of their evidence is that flow of water from the glacier was very small during a surge, so it was presumed to be trapped under the ice. After a surge, flow of water from the glacier was very voluminous for a short time as the stored water escaped.

There can be no doubt of an association between high water levels and high water pressures and the surge movement. The question is which is the cause and which is the effect, even if we allow that either one is the cause, because the two phenomena may be an effect of another cause as yet unknown.

I think it is worthwhile to examine the whole surge picture again to understand what observations need explanation. Kamb and the others have shown the association of surge movement with high water pressure under and within the glacier. Certainly the mechanism of movement must be tied into the water somehow. If we want to understand the whole surge mechanism, not just the actual rapid movement, then we must look at the whole interval between one surge event and the next one.

The concept of energy storage in natural buffers as a cause of periodic geologic events provides a useful framework. Stored energy is released after a period that is proportional to the size of the storage buffer and to the rate at which energy accumulates in the buffer. Energy is released from a buffer when a natural threshold is exceeded or when release is triggered by some external cause. The released energy typically follows a pattern of small releases over a time prior to major release. Then energy is released in episodes during which there is rapid acceleration of release to a peak followed by decay to background levels. Major releases may consist of several events.

The surge-glacier phenomenon seems to fit the buffer model perfectly, and we might ask, What is the buffer? The period for Variegated Glacier is seventeen to twenty years. What sort of energy is stored over that period?

It is implicit in the buffer paradigm that the cause, and hence the buffer, is inherently a part of the phenomenon, so the buffer for surge glaciers is most likely the glacier itself. Unfortunately, Variegated Glacier wasn't placed under close scrutiny during the whole period from 1965 to 1983, but Kamb and company did start in 1973, so we have a record of a decade during which energy storage was taking place.

Energy can be stored in various forms such as heat, as with geysers or volcanoes, or elastic strain, as with earthquakes. It would seem that heat is not stored in a glacier. We shall see about that later. Is storage of elastic strain a reasonable expectation for a plastic substance such as ice? Energy can be stored as potential energy—the energy that matter possesses if it can move to a lower energy state. Glaciers are, by definition, buffers that store potential energy in that they are bodies that are under the influence of gravity and are not at the lowest possible topographical level.

I have emphasized the plastic nature of ice, but ice does have some rigidity. In other words, there is a threshold of stress for ice below which it behaves as a rigid substance. Thus, a glacier that is stable or moving slowly down a valley is a buffer that contains a store of potential energy that is proportional to its volume and its height above its terminus. In addition, the glacier buffer does contain stored elastic strain because it supports its own weight. It has strength. Even on a small scale the ice contains bubbles of air under compression, so there is elastic strain in the ice and in the bubbles.

Kamb and his co-workers observed that from year to year the ice in Variegated Glacier was thickening in the middle and upper reaches, comprising roughly the upper half of the glacier, and thinning in the lower portion. In buffer terms, the buffer was becoming filled with energy because ice in the upper half was not only thicker but at a higher potential energy state than in the lower half. The total stored energy was certainly increasing from 1973 onward, when their study began, and it is likely fair to assume that it had been doing so since the close of the 1965 surge events.

The seventeen- to twenty-year periodicity of surging by Variegated tells us that a threshold for spontaneous energy release was being approached in the late 1970s. Kamb and company had observed as early as 1973 that the ice mass was at the melting point throughout, so there was not an effect of raising of temperature, but we might wonder if the total ratio of water to ice was increasing by progressive melting and storage of water in the glacier. An increase in the water/ice ratio would mean a storage of energy as heat as well as potential and elastic energy because heat is consumed in the melting of ice even though the temperature remains at the melting temperature.

During the energy-storage interval, the ice movement increased steadily, but not at a great enough rate to leak off the stored energy. In 1978–81 energy began to be released in the minisurges, forerunners of the big release to come.

Then, in 1982, a major threshold was exceeded, and the buffer was emptied in a series of large events. In the emptying process, ice moved from the upper half to the lower half, setting the buffer to zero. We can fairly assume that the process of buffer filling is now once again going on, leading to another surge event at the turn of the century.

The exact mechanism of the surge release is still unknown. Kamb and his friends have proposed one possibility wherein water is trapped in cavities connected by small openings so that flow is restricted and pressure builds up. I prefer a mechanism such as one proposed by USGS geologist Rudolph Kopf wherein the pressure of a solid mass onto sediment-laden water causes pressure increases, the pressure being confined by the sediment plugging or restricting possible exits. Certainly there is some mechanism whereby water trapped in and under the glacier and the combined weight of the ice and water causes a failure of catastrophic proportions at or near the point when the pressure of the water exceeds the weight of the overlying material. Whether one puts the finger on the water or the ice as the culprit is probably irrelevant. It is the fact that both ice and water are stored in an unstable state that sets up the surge.

It is the periodicity of surge events that tells us that energy storage is involved in the overall structure of the phenomenon. One can hope that Variegated Glacier and other surge glaciers will be studied throughout a full cycle so that all the pieces of the mystery can be assembled.

Why don't all glaciers behave that way? Nobody knows why, but it is observed that ordinary glaciers thicken or became thin throughout their length and do not get thicker at the top and thinner at the bottom and that the position of the terminus shifts up and down valley in response to changes in the total mass of the glacier. Surge glaciers don't behave as units in that sense, so there is the opportunity for energy differences to increase between the upper portion and lower portions. Ordinary glaciers somehow adjust more rapidly, which is to say that they do not comprise competent buffers, because storable energy leaks away almost as it accumulates. That is reflected in the fact that most glaciers advance as ice is removed from the terminus, either falling into the sea, the so-called calving, or breaking off on land and melting. Surge glaciers don't do that. The ice at the terminus of a surge glacier is so-called dead ice. It just sits there and melts without advancing or breaking off. Surge glaciers must be more rigid for some reason, perhaps because of a difference in the proportions of ice, air, and mineral grains or in the relations of one ice grain to another. Certainly there are reasons just waiting for some scientist to discover. Let's hope Kamb and his colleagues get funding to keep up their work and that others will join in looking at other surge glaciers.

I for one am saving my pennies to go up to Variegated Glacier as soon as the word gets out that the minisurges are beginning again. It gives a good excuse to go see Alaska in any case, and it seems a shame to let all that stored energy just go away unnoticed by appreciative eyes. I'll see you in Alaska right around the year 2000. Don't forget your camera and a pair of sturdy boots.

CHAPTER **THREE**

From Order to Chaos and Back Again— A Case of Misunderstanding

In the seventeenth century, Nicolas Steno, the wide-ranging Dane also know as Niels Steensen, noticed that the angles between comparable faces of quartz crystals were the same, irrespective of the shape of the crystals. That observation, confirmed by others and later elevated in stature to the law of the constancy of interfacial angles, has had long-term effects on the thinking of mineralogists and other crystallographers. It has even had what might be called a stifling influence. It was a rule so profound, so all encompassing, that it both stimulated research and set limits for the discipline of the understanding of solids.

It is often the nature of great ideas to send thinkers in pursuit of fresh horizons armed with a new insight or framework to unravel the mysteries of the world—to pursue god if you will. Thus it was that Steno's observation was carried along by others who concluded that the message from the law of constancy of interfacial angles was that crystalline solids were built up of fundamental parts that were stacked in an orderly, repetitive array. This was a reasonable, and one could say, revolutionary assumption.

The idea that layers or three-dimensional arrays of objects
arranged in a mathematically perfect order could explain
the diversity of shapes of natural objects was embraced with
ardor by the numerically inclined.

Mineralogists later discovered that all natural crystals be-
longed to one or another of a family of thirty-two crystal
shapes called crystal classes. No exceptions were found to
that rule. It was also discovered that such solids could be
described within a set of rules based on the mathematical
repetition of points in three-dimensional space. Generations
of scientists were trained to keep the faith. The faith was
that all solids were made up of particles that were arranged
according to laws describing all the ways that anything
could be arrayed by what are called symmetry operations.

Symmetry operations are a conceptual term for the
equivalence of one or more points or objects. The most
familiar symmetry operation is that of mirror symmetry.
The left shoe is the mirror image of the right, or the left
ear is the mirror version of the right ear.

Another symmetry operation is translation, one often
used in printing wallpaper or gift wrap in which the same
pattern or picture is repeated over and over again on a
roll of paper. Another is rotation. For example, if a cube
is rotated around an imaginary axis that joins the centers
of two opposite square sides, the cube will appear the same
every one-quarter of a complete revolution about the axis.
That element is called a fourfold axis. It is gospel, and
can be rather easily proved, that there are only onefold,
twofold, threefold, fourfold, and sixfold axes of rotational
symmetry for regular repetitive arrays of points.

There are thirty-two ways of arranging the various simple
symmetry elements of a regular array of points that corre-
spond to the thirty-two crystal classes. If additional symmetry
elements are introduced and if the repetitive points themselves have no symmetry, like a lumpy potato instead of a
little sphere, there are 230 arrangements of real objects,
called space groups.

There is a universal loveliness in the laws of crystallography that appeals to mineralogist, physicist, and biologist alike. It is a safe world in which there are no surprises—only new modifications of the same themes, a world of slight variations among the familiar. It's a world in which a doctorate and even a whole career can be explored in the security that the theory will pick up your apples if you do everything right. It's Mom.

The universal belief in the concept that real, crystalline solids were made up of atoms ordered according to the unbending rules of the possible arrangements of symmetry elements got its strength from the fact that the concept had never failed the test. An idea in science must be testable in some of many ways, and only after it has been challenged by many tests does it become accepted by the practitioners of science as a working theory or a law. At first a few, then dozens, then hundreds and thousands of natural and artificial crystalline substances were examined by optical means, with X rays, beams of particles, electrical currents, heat-transmission properties, and on and on, and all of the results reinforced the concept of order of the atoms in solids according to the rules. It became completely axiomatic that any crystalline arrangement fit into one of the 230 space-group arrangements. If any data disagreed, it was back to the lab to see what sort of mistake might have been made, because with crystal structure there was no room for originality on the part of either crystals or crystallographers.

To give you some idea of the depth of belief, let me quote from some respected authorities in the field. M. J. Buerger of M.I.T., the dean of American crystallographers, wrote in his book *Elementary Crystallography*—a title which redefines the meaning of the word "elementary"—as follows: "Since crystals are regions of matter composed of the same kind of molecule systematically repeated, these must be arranged in one of the 230 three-dimensional pattern types." R. C. Evans of Cambridge University wrote in his important book *Crystal Chemistry*, with reference to X-ray studies confirming earlier speculations about crystal structures: "The crystal structures . . . were elucidated, and . . . the general principles underlying the structural characteristics of all known types of solid matter had become clear."

I think it is significant that crystallography as we know it began in Europe and the West. A predilection for belief in symmetry of things and events is a characteristic of Western peoples and cultures. We see it in architecture, poetry, politics, and machines—indeed in almost every element of our lives. The angles between the edges of paper are universally 90 degrees, and it is unthinkable that it could be otherwise. The size of the left shoe is the exact mirror-image duplicate of the left, even though with most of us the right foot is larger than the left. There are endless examples, but the point is that it is not necessary that everything in the world possess some obvious symmetry.

In Eastern cultures symmetry is not so important as in the West. Lack of symmetry is an important part of Zen. Objects in the Zen world should lack symmetry, just as the natural world lacks symmetry. Left is not exactly the same as right any more than yesterday is the same as tomorrow. A Japanese garden is arranged to look asymmetrical by artful landscapers. An English garden is beaten into symmetry by equally artful caretakers. A bowl from a British or German factory is perfectly shaped, with no variation from the circular cross section at any cut parallel to its base. A Japanese raiku bowl is intentionally made asymmetrical by being picked out of the kiln with tongs while the hot silicate mass is still plastic. Each Western bowl is, ideally, just the same as every other. After all, the bride wants all her presents to match. Each raiku bowl is obviously unique, just as each carrot or tree or rock or person is unique.

One could wonder what would have happened if crystallography had its start in a Zen environment. However, it did not, and the whole world, including scientists from the East, believed in the doctrine of the space groups.

Given a new, unstudied crystal, a crystallographer, whether mineralogist, chemist, physicist, biologist, or other practitioner, makes somes preliminary determination of symmetry properties. If an exquisite little crystal with sparkling faces is available, then the external morphology gives a toehold on the problem. Lacking that, there are various physical tests that are used. Then the crystal is studied by X rays. As it happens, the spacing between atoms in a crystal is about the same order of magnitude as the wavelength of X rays. This means that the X rays are scattered in coherent ways by a crystal and can be used to infer the arrangement of the atoms in the crystal. Other methods are used for determination of crystal structures, but for the most part, a gross examination usually places the arrangement into one of the 32 so-called point groups, and the X-ray analysis (called X-ray diffraction) pigeon-holes the crystal arrangement into one or more possibilities among the 230 space groups.

At that point the procedure consists of various ways of determining what arrangement of actual atoms conforms to the space-group symmetry. The procedure may be very simple or may be horribly complex and difficult, involving many years and many scientists, but it is basically cut-and-dried—get the space group and fit the atoms into it.

As I mentioned previously, no exceptions to this fitting of nature into the concept of symmetry groups had ever been found. Perhaps it is more realistic to state that no exceptions had ever been reported in the scientific literature. A crystallographer who found data that didn't fit the scheme would have just assumed that a mistake of some sort had been made. If the anomalous work was shown to a colleague or a superior, there would be strong objections and a questioning of the worker's competency. If an article describing the crystal that didn't fit the rules was submitted to a journal, it would surely be rejected. One can assume that an innocent and eager graduate student discovering a violation of the space-group dogma and telling a professor about it would suffer career termination. Almost all research scientists were once graduate students, so the pressure to make no waves is pervasive.

It was in this setting, in 1982, that Daniel Shechtman, on leave from the Israel Institute of Technology, was making routine X-ray diffraction studies of newly developed aluminum-manganese alloys at the National Bureau of Standards in Gaithersburg, Maryland. Dr. Shechtman found the unthinkable. He found fivefold symmetry. He knew that was impossible. He checked and rechecked his work. It was for real.

What he found was an arrangement that gave rise to a solid figure called an icosahedron that had faces with ordinary twofold and threefold symmetry, but also with some of the forbidden fivefold kind. I realize that an icosahedron is not the sort of object that leaps into the mind's eye, but there are examples of that and other "noncrystallographic" figures all around us. They reached their peak a few years past during the hippie movement and are familiar at avant garde shopping malls and world's fairs. They are geodesic domes, Buckminster Fuller's great contribution to architecture and children's playground toys. Many of Fuller's domes have faces with fivefold symmetry.

I greeted early reports of Shechtman's discovery with suspicion, then amazement, then pleasure. The pleasure was because my wife and I had built a fourteen-sided house and I, the designer, had been given a bit of flak by colleagues, who chided me, a teacher of crystallography, for the sin of building a house with incorrect symmetry—at least incorrect for a student of crystals. Now here was a real crystal that disdained the rule of only one-, two- three-, four-, and sixfold symmetry, so my fourteen wasn't so outrageous, after all.

Shechtman's work was confirmed by other laboratories, so rather than being drummed out of the corps of scientists in disgrace, he was respected for his discovery. His discovery, like many in science, resulted from noticing the out of the ordinary. Recognizing anomalous things is an important step in scientific research, and it is an advantage that experienced workers have over younger scientists. The youngster, however bright, simply may not have enough experience and stored information to recognize the usual from the unusual. In this case, however, the anomaly was the sort of thing that even a mediocre student in sophomore mineralogy or a similar-level course in other natural sciences would be expected to recognize. Shechtman's advantage was more in the line of self-confidence, persistence, and guts.

Why, we might ask, has it taken until now for this discovery, and how did the dogma of 230 space groups become so entrenched? It clearly happened because of the sequence of concepts that led to crystallography as a science. First was Steno's observation that interfacial angles were constant for a given set of crystals of the same material. That led to the concept that crystals were made up of tiny bodies that were stacked together to make a whole crystal. Such bodies must have shapes such that they fill space, leaving no voids. Such bodies can also be shown to have only 32 point groups or 230 space-group symmetries. Thus, crystallography as a science took less account of the properties of the actual atoms in a crystal, and how those might limit possible arrangements, than of the abstract geometry of relations among points in space.

Let's go back to filling space without voids in case that one left you puzzled. We can consider some two-dimensional examples. A visit to the tile store, at least mentally, is useful. Tiles are manufactured either rectangular, square, or six sided. Such tiles show, respectively, twofold, fourfold, or sixfold symmetry. Such tiles can also be placed together to fill space on the kitchen counter or bathroom floor. Although I've never seen such on the commercial market, one could also fill space with a set of identical parallelograms or triangles with two or more sides equal. Unlike the other tiles, the triangles would have to be rotated with respect to their neighbors to fill space. One cannot fill space with tiles that have fivefold, sevenfold, eightfold, or higher symmetry without leaving gaps.

Because of this intuitively obvious fact and the concept of stacking tiny minicrystals (called unit cells) to make real crystals, the existence of fivefold, sevenfold, and higher rotational symmetry was eliminated at the starting gate. The "book" response to Shechtman would be that icosahedrons couldn't be stacked to fill space and thus the structure was impossible. The real point is that the unit-cell concept needed reexamination.

In spite of the social barriers to discovering a violation of the symmetry rules, it does seem strange that it took so long to happen. One reason it did is that lots of real crystals presumably do actually conform to the rules exactly. Another is that determination of crystal structure is not a precise science. In real crystals the atoms are in constant motion, and real crystals are also actually mosaics of small domains with a certain amount of disorder superimposed on the order of the individual domains. Because of these facts and a plethora of others, a crystal structure is only known approximately at best. Thus, many crystal-structure determinations may well be a matter of fitting the data to the closest approximation space-group symmetry. The crystal is assigned to a space group, but in reality there certainly are minor departures from the ideal arrangement. If we knew the *exact* arrangement in natural crystals, we might find that most of them didn't conform perfectly to an ideal arrangement according to group theory.

Such a statement would have been heresy before Shechtman and would probably raise hackles on many a crystallographer even after Shechtman. A realistic view in hindsight is Why should crystals be made up of regular periodic arrays of atoms? Why indeed, because there is a much more fundamental rule that governs the arrangement of atoms in a crystal. That rule is that the arrangement must be one that results in a low-energy state. Each atom must be in a relationship with all its neighbors such that the total energy of the crystal is at a minimum. This truly fundamental constraint on crystal structures is unrelated to space-group symmetry.

Obviously a space-group arrangement, or a close approximation of it, must be also a minimum-energy arrangement for most crystalline substances, so the myth persisted for a long time. Now the smug professors will have to modify their lectures. I suspect that most of them will still teach the same dogma as ever with a mumbled aside in a lecture or a fine-print footnote in a book to the extent that there are *very* rare exceptions to the rules.

One can sympathize. Crystallographers have lived so long under the beautiful and perfect umbrella of order—order without exception—that they will be loath to part with it. They won't want to take that first step away from what they've believed in. It's like a wool grower wearing a polyester suit or a vegetarian sampling some meat. It's like a fundamentalist questioning one sentence or verse in a holy book. It leads to chaos.

Of course it is not chaos at all. It's just that crystals don't grow according to geometry. They grow according to the fundamental physical laws of the natural world, the laws that govern everything, and especially the law that every process in nature, including crystallization, proceeds in the direction of lowering of energy. What could be more orderly than that?

Shechtman's work was not published until late 1984, but by July 1985 a team of Japanese scientists had published a short note about a nickel-chromium alloy with twelvefold symmetry, and others, including D. R. Nelson and B. I. Halperin of Harvard's Lyman Laboratory, had found five-fold symmetry in other aluminum alloys. Workers in laboratories all over the world are digging old data out of the files in which anomalies are kept in semisecret storage.

No doubt many "noncrystallographic" crystals will be found when data are accepted at face value rather than forced into the mold of the space groups. Scientific papers will be written; new ideas will be presented at meetings. Textbooks and lectures will be revised—sometimes reluctantly.

At present dual Nobelist Linus Pauling is defending the faith and insisting that Shechtman's "quasicrystals," as Pauling calls them, are the result of the regular growth of twenty separate ordinary crystals which interlock to produce the fivefold symmetry from a special kind of aggregate crystal that crystallographers called twinned. John W. Cahn of the National Bureau of Standards first told Schechtman "Go away, Danny, that's just twinning" and then, later, coauthored the first publication. At present Cahn, Nelson, Halperin, and others are taking the side that Pauling's pseudocrystals or twins are real crystals, as Pauling builds his case for twinning. It may be a while before a consensus is reached, but such is the stuff of science. Pauling is one of my personal heros and it puts my emotions on the line because my great respect for him makes me want to believe in twinning as the explanation, but the heretic in me leads me in the direction of icosahedral crystals. Tests will be devised and one side or theory or the other will emerge as the favorite. Whatever the outcome, the controversy is a good one in that it challenges one of the foundation stones of the whole span of science. Scientists in every discipline will be reminded that there is no such thing as truth or proof—and that's a healthy thing.

CHAPTER FOUR

Boron 93516

The lad had finally been given the controls after acting as navigator for the whole trip. He had kept hoping that his father would give him a chance ever since they left the last fuel stop and pointed the vehicle on its course. They had also taken on water and supplies and made checks of fluid levels and air pressure at the stop, because a trip to 93516 was a serious matter, with no room for mistakes. Even on a family outing one had to take the usual precautions.

He felt nervous but was pleased that he held the vehicle steady and that his father made only minimal comments about his technique. At least they were out of the cruising range of the officials who might intercept them and ask to see if the boy had a license. Oh, the patrols could come out here if they chose, but almost nobody came this way, so they stayed nearer to home or scanned the busy routes to distant places like 89114 and 92363. At the pair's destination, 93516, or Boron, as some called it, there was no excitement for the patrols, so they avoided that duty. Boron just barely sustained human life, much less excitement. Workers there put in extra time in order to get furloughs back to less hostile worlds.

The boy cruised at reduced speed to conserve fuel as well as to cope with his inexperience at the controls. They skirted the restricted zone where military craft and weapons were tested, and finally, far in the distance, looking like a speck in the nothingness, was Boron, illuminated by pale orange sunlight.

Boron grew larger and larger, and finally they could see the great pit in the surface and the dusty buildings and machinery. Great trucks rumbled back and forth in clouds of dust. Boron was a waterless place, and the dust clouds blew back and forth with every change in the hot, dry atmosphere. As they approached the parking apron near the factory, the father took the controls just in case there was a patrol there. The engine shuddered to a stop, and the boy and his father stepped out into the intense sunlight and dry, yellow atmosphere of Boron 93516. The place was not like Earth at all.

They had traveled here to see if they could get some specimens of the rare minerals found there for the boy's collection; 93516 was given the name Boron because it contained a great store of the element boron. The element boron only makes up about ten parts per million of Earth's crust, but at the Boron mines there were great masses of borates mined, processed, and sent to Earth cities in great gondolas. The boy marveled that there could be so much of such a rare element in one place. He remembered reading that the cosmic abundance of boron was one billionth that of hydrogen. He was excited to be at such a place.

That tale isn't science fiction. The lad in the story was I, and 93516 isn't the catalog number of a distant planet but the ZIP code of the town of Boron, California, the location of the world's largest borate mine. Boron is now just a short distance off a four-lane freeway, but when I went there with my father in the 1940s, it was a very remote place—as described—in the Mojave Desert of Southern California. One did make sure to have enough fuel and water when venturing into the desert, all the more so because wartime gasoline rationing made traffic scarce and far between.

It is also a fact that boron is a rare element and that the deposits at Boron accounted for essentially all of the world's commercial supply of that element until recent discoveries in Turkey. There are a few small deposits elsewhere, notably in Argentina, but they are very small compared to the great Boron deposits and those in Turkey. I emphasize this because therein lies a geologic mystery that bears some investigation. Why should such a rare element be so concentrated in just two places?

In order to pursue these and related questions, we should look at the chemical and geochemical properties of boron to get some insight into its behavior in geologic settings. As the boy knew, boron only makes up about ten parts per million, or 0.001 percent, of the outer part of the earth. At Boron there are great masses of a mineral that contains sixteen thousand times as much as the average crust. Put another way, all the boron in a slab of ordinary rock 250 feet thick and over 1,200 square miles in area is concentrated in a 250-foot-thick layer less than a square mile in area at Boron. Moreover, there are extensive deposits of boron minerals and boron-rich brines in the immediate region of Boron, so the magnitude of the accumulation is even greater than one would surmise from the size of the deposit processed at Boron.

How, then, did these extraordinary deposits come to be? First of all, the borates are in thick (up to 90 feet) layers of sodium borates separated by minor layers of shale. They are typical of so-called evaporite deposits, that is, deposits of soluble salts that precipitated and crystallized from brines produced by the evaporation of water. The evaporites are underlain by dark basalt lava flows and overlain by coarse-grained sandstones. The only nonevaporite sedimentary rocks in the borate-bearing sequence are the clay stones and some thin volcanic ash layers.

A geologist looking at the sequence would imagine the

history of the deposit to be something such as a shallow basin developing in the basalt flows, possibly through downwarping or faulting of the surface rocks. That basin then must have become a lake as surface waters accumulated, with no exit from the shallow pan. The relief of the terrain must have been very low, and hence the lake relatively large and shallow, because the sediments interlayered with the borates are exclusively fine-grained clays without silt or sand-sized particles. Clays can be transported in suspension in quietly moving water, while silt and sand require swifter bottom currents. The volcanic ashes were deposited directly from the air. Lake currents were sluggish enough for much of the time that only pure borates were deposited, with not even any suspended clay mixed in. It is suggestive that the climate was arid inasmuch as a lot of water must have evaporated to leave all the borates. It may well be that the clay layers represent wet climate cycles when evaporation was less and more clay-rich water was able to flow out into the center of the lake. We can imagine a large, shallow lake with sandy margins and extensive mud flats with a small area of open water in the center. In dry weather the mud flats would be cracked and hard, like modern dry lakes in the desert. Water may have flowed lazily to the central part of the lake bed, but it carried little or no sediment, only dissolved materials. In times of heavy rains or wet climate intervals, sand would have been swept onto the mud flats by vigorous sheet floods and turbulent streams. The sands would have been deposited around the margins as the currents slackened, but only the suspended clays were carried all the way to the saline brines in the center of the basin to form the clay layers in the borate evaporites. At the top of the evaporites the successive rock layers are clays with some minor borates, followed by clays and then sandstones. That final sequence tells us that either the basin deepened or the climate became wetter, or both, because the deposition by evaporation became overwhelmed by the influx of successively coarser sediments. Fossils found in the overlying claystones are of mammals of middle Miocene age, so we can imagine that the climate in the region was not much different, unless perhaps a bit more arid, fifteen to twenty million years ago than it is now.

So we can interpret the sequence to get a picture of a desert lake with broad mud flats and a central brine pond. That's all very well, but why borate brines? If we look at modern desert lakes, there are a few with minor borates, but most of them have brines and evaporite layers made up the mineral halite—sodium chloride—or common table salt. Others, especially those in the rift valley in Kenya and adjacent countries, are sodium carbonate lakes. Many lakes also have layers composed of calcium and magnesium carbonates. This is clearly a complex business.

The first evaporites to be studied were the ones at Stassfurt, Germany, and nearby areas which have been mined for many centuries. Those deposits result from evaporation of seawater rather than inland lake waters, but they carry some important lessons. Geologists and chemists attempting to understand the Stassfurt deposits studied evaporation of seawater and found that with evaporation the first solids to crystallize would be calcite and dolomite, calcium and calcium-magnesium carbonates. With further concentration gypsum, calcium sulfate comes out, then halite, then in the last salts, potassium and magnesium sulfates. Some minor amounts of boron-containing minerals accompany the last salts.

The sequence of deposition of salts is related to a number of factors, with solubility, concentration in solution, and temperature of great influence. All else being equal, a salt of low solubility will be expected to precipitate early as is the case with seawater, with limestones and dolomites coming out first, followed by the somewhat more soluble gypsum. Concentration is a factor, too, of course, because even a substance of low solubility will remain in solution if its quantity is small. Temperature influences solubility,

so, it, too, can have major effects. For example, the salts
that crystallize from Great Salt Lake in Utah are different
in winter than in summer. The process of crystallization
results in continuous changes in the concentration of various dissolved substances as the brine composition changes
in response to removal of crystallizing materials. The whole
process whereby different salts are deposited at different
stages and minor salts become concentrated in successive
residues is called fractional crystallization and is used in
commercial processes to isolate pure salts in imitation of
nature.

Boron is comparatively rare in evaporites from seawater.
It occurs in the most highly fractionated deposits, and there
in tiny amounts. Borates also occur in the last salts to
precipitate, because they are very soluble. There is another
reason, however, for the rarity. Boron is an element that is
chemically attracted to marine sediments, especially the
clay portion. Thus, saltwater is impoverished in boron
relative to its relative abundance. The same is true for
potassium, which is why the sea is rich in sodium but contains relatively little potassium, at least when compared
to the abundance of potassium in river waters entering the
sea.

Sodium chloride is a major constituent of most inland
evaporites, as epitomized by Great Salt Lake, Utah, where
evaporation in artificial ponds is used to produce commercial halite. At Bristol Lake in the Mojave Desert solid
crystalline halite is mined from a brine-crystal mixture.
Both these lakes and others contain other soluble materials,
but sodium chloride is a major salt. It is generally assumed
that chloride lakes derived a major portion of their salts
from old seawater. When marine sediments are aggregated
together and formed into layers of sedimentary rock, there
is much pore space that is occupied by seawater. That water
remains in the rock until it is flushed out by moving
groundwater or removed when the rock is weathered at the
surface. The old seawater may appear in springs at the

surface or enter the surface waters through weathering. Either way, sodium chloride can become trapped in inland bodies of water to form chloride-rich lakes.

Many other lakes are relatively chloride-poor, with carbonates prevailing. Until a few years ago the carbonate lakes were a bit of a puzzle. Not that carbonate isn't common; all surface waters contain dissolved carbonate from the carbon dioxide in the air. The puzzling thing was that so many lakes contain almost all sodium carbonates when surface waters contain lots of dissolved calcium carbonate, as well. The answer came from a number of studies, but perhaps the most seminal were made in the African rift valley by Hans Eugster of Johns Hopkins. Eugster studied the waters entering the rift basin from springs and found that they were sodium-carbonate waters. He looked at the waters on the surfaces above the rift valleys and found that they were more or less normal surface waters without an abnormal enrichment in sodium carbonate. Something happened to the water between the time it entered the ground and the time it emerged from springs in the rift valley below. The answer was that the calcium carbonate was deposited in openings in the rocks on the way down as the mineral calcite, leaving a relative enrichment in sodium carbonate. This process has now been observed in many geologic situations.

Groundwater that percolates downward through the coarse sands and gravels that flank desert mountains starts out as ordinary surface water and then emerges as sodium-carbonate-rich water. Many soda lakes of the western part of the United States owe their origin to such a history. Other soda lakes derive their sodium carbonate from weathering of the common mineral plagioclase feldspar (a sodium-calcium aluminosilicate) in shales. In the weathering process, the calcium stays behind as calcium sulfate (gypsum) by combining with sulfate released by weathering of iron sulfide (pyrite) in the shales, and the sodium is removed in solution to lakes.

Boron minerals are generally absent in nonmarine evaporites except for a few occurrences. In Searles Lake, located about 50 miles north of Boron, boron minerals occur along with a great variety of other evaporite minerals. Also, there are various borate occurrences in Death Valley and other areas in the general region.

Whence the boron? Boron is concentrated in marine sediments, where it is tightly bound to clay minerals. When such sediments are subjected to burial and heating deep within the crust of the earth, two sorts of things happen. In the case of heating below the melting point of the rocks, they may become transformed into new rocks—metamorphic rocks—through the breakdown of old minerals and the formation of new ones that are more stable in the high temperature and pressure conditions. Under such conditions much of the boron enters into a complex silicate mineral called tourmaline. Tourmaline is a highly stable mineral under a wide range of physical and chemical conditions. For example, it is insoluble in hydrofluoric acid, an acid that readily dissolves quartz, window glass, and almost all natural silicates. In addition to being unreactive, tourmaline is hard and tough and resists abrasion and breakage. Thus, once boron is locked up in tourmaline, it is pretty much taken out of circulation—literally—and no longer is available in the geochemical environment as a dissolved substance.

The great geochemist V. M. Goldschmidt noted that boron is more abundant in old marine sediments than in younger ones, and he suggests that the boron content of seawater has decreased through geologic time. If that is true—and some scientists don't agree with Goldschmidt—we could attribute it to the tying up of boron in marine shales and then further locking up of it in tourmaline in metamorphic rocks, whence it is unavailable as a soluble component of surface waters.

When boron-bearing marine sediments are deeply buried, they can be melted, especially in subduction zones, places where slabs of crust are pushed under other slabs as crustal plates move about. Under conditions of melting rather than recrystallization the boron is not tied up in tourmaline but remains mobile in the melted rock. This rock can rise to the surface as lava or may form shallow underground bodies that cool more slowly beneath the surface.

Volcanic activity, whether it reaches the surface to form volcanoes and lava flows or whether it remains underground, is generally associated with hot springs, geysers, and steam vents. In many parts of the world, boron minerals are deposited around such hot-water vents, and there is even minor commercial production of borates in Tuscany, Italy. Perhaps the boron that formed the deposits at Boron was of volcanic origin.

Certainly at Boron, the deposit is underlain by basalt lava flows, and there are volcanic ash layers in the borate layers and above the deposit. Indeed, from a variety of geologic evidence, the whole region during Miocene time was subject to much volcanic activity. There is similar volcanic and hot-spring association in Turkey, Iran, Tibet, Argentina, Bolivia, Peru, and Chile as well as other parts of the western United States.

Important contributions from a hot-spring source for borate deposits is almost required, because there is seemingly no other way that surface waters could contain large amounts of dissolved boron without also containing even larger amounts of chloride, calcium, potassium, and other common elements found in inland evaporites. Normal weathering cannot produce boron-rich waters. Even at Searles Lake, north of Boron, the amount of borates in the evaporites and brines is abnormally large in the extreme. Thus, borate lakes must be supplied largely by water from hot springs, with very minor contributions from ordinary surface flow. Also, calcium borates are relatively insoluble (the Turkish deposits are calcium borates and of a different origin than those at Boron), so the water system must have been low in calcium, much like the calcium-poor

waters in the African rift valley or in many sodium carbonate lakes in the United States. This geochemical re-
quirements suggest a very arid climate without important
surface drainage. In addition, ancient Lake Boron may
have been one of a chain of shallow lakes so that many
salts were precipitated in an upstream lake and never
reached Lake Boron. Such was the case with nearby Searles
Lake, which was the third in a series of lakes, thereby containing the most soluble of the various dissolved salts, because the less soluble ones were removed in the first two
lakes before the water got to Searles Lake. Natural fractionation again. The fractionation must have been even
more extreme for Lake Boron inasmuch as the evaporites
there are essentially pure borates. Calcium salts must have
been removed early either during underground flow or in
upstream lakes. Even the sodium and potassium sulfates
and carbonates must have likewise been greatly reduced
so that the most concentrated material was sodium borate:
a combination of fractionation and a major contribution of
borate-rich spring water.

In the South American occurrences, the borates are generally accompanied by nitrates. Nitrates are highly soluble
in water and can accumulate only in extremely arid regions.
The Asiatic deposits are accompanied by ammonia salts,
also very soluble and preserved only in the virtual absence
of rain.

So it seems that the mystery is pretty much solved. The
Boron deposits accumulated in a closed desert basin that
was fed by hot springs and probably by periodic overflow
from other desert lakes. The climate was probably highly
arid, and except from other lakes surface drainage failed
to reach prehistoric Lake Boron. There have been no fossils
reported from rocks within the ore body. The fossils that
date the occurrence are from rocks overlying the borates.
Perhaps the local climate was too inhospitable to support
much life during the dry-lake episode, mammals moved
into the area only after the dryness moderated, and surface

drainage brought in the sediments in which fossils have been found. Indeed, an area in which the only water sources were boron-rich would not only be inhospitable; it would be downright deadly. Boron compounds are fairly poisonous, a fact that should be remembered when boric acid is used to bathe baby's eyes or when a name-brand commercial boron compound made popular by a former actor turned politician is added to the laundry water. As with most things, boron, actors, politicians, and babies are best when experienced in moderation. Too much of any of them can make an environment hostile, if not downright toxic.

CHAPTER FIVE

The Coral Clock and Other Lines of Evidence

In the mythology of the Greeks many of the characters were created full grown, without the need to develop by slow steps, as with most mortals. The view that objects were created fully formed was likewise used to explain the finding of stony objects that strongly resembled modern, living, shelled organisms in rock layers far removed from seas or rivers. We are told in countless textbooks that religious leaders of the time taught that such objects were placed in rocks to confuse man's search for knowledge and to test his faith in God.

To my knowledge, it is not recorded to what extent the average person accepted that view, although it is taken for fact that being a heretic was not a pleasant pastime for much of recorded history. A not-so-average person, Leonardo da Vinci, was not persuaded by the dogma and wrote:

> And if you were to say that these shells were created, and were continually being created in such places by the nature of the spot, and of the heavens which might have some influence there, such an opinion cannot exist in a brain of much reason; because here are the years of their growth, numbered on their shells, and there are large ones and small

ones to be seen which could not have grown without food, and could not have fed without motion—and here they could not move.

Leonardo struck two blows for science and common sense in his statement by correctly recognizing that the shells were remains of once-living ceatures whose stages of growth were recorded as changes in form of the surfaces of the shells. Two centuries later, in the 1600s, Nicolas Steno was still trying to convince people that shark-tooth-like objects in the rocks of Italy were really the teeth of extinct sharks. Learning comes slowly.

The presence of indicators of growth in the tissues of some organisms was surely not open to serious argument even in Leonardo's time. Wood had been a familiar material to everyone for thousands of years both as a material for building as well as a major fuel. The rings of growth as seen in a cross section of a tree trunk or branch were no doubt correctly interpreted as annual growth increments by even the least sophisticated peasants.

People living near the sea could also hardly fail to notice that the shells of clams and other bivalves show growth lines formed as the animals increased in size. A thoughtful person would have even noticed that the growth lines on a typical clam are ordered, with groups of many finely spaced lines set off from other groups by major divisions. Such major divisions could be interpreted as annual divisions, and the age of the clam determined thereby.

The use of increments or stages of growth to determine age of organisms is a widespread practice in a variety of disciplines and fields of endeavor. The age of a domestic sheep can be estimated from the yearly replacement of baby teeth by permanent ones. With horned sheep and other horned animals there are growth lines on the horns that show annual and less lengthy stages in their formation. With horses the use of teeth for estimating age is celebrated in the old expression about the social error of looking a

gift horse in the mouth. Indeed, periodic features are seen
on the hard parts of many animals: lines on the shells of
turtles and on scales of fish, rattles on rattlesnakes, layers in
pearls—the list is almost endless. It is, however, a giant step
to move from recognition of periodic structures to using
them for estimation of age or other properties of the organism, because one has no *a priori* way of determining the
time interval represented by a growth line or even whether
a line in a given group of lines was caused by the same
process as other lines in the same group.

With tree rings the evidence of annual rings is strongly
suggestive, and their annual nature can be proved readily
by simply planting a tree and counting the rings a few
years later. Because of this easily testable theory, tree-ring
counting became a popular pastime of woodsman and
scientist alike. The scientific side of looking at tree rings
is now given the erudite name of dendrochronology when
it is used to determine age and is widely used for a variety
of purposes.

Although the rings in wood are generally annual, there are
other factors that make the rings more useful than one might
imagine. For one thing, the width of the rings is dependent
on environmental conditions such as availability of water,
ambient temperature, availability of mineral nutrients, and
various other factors. Thus, a given sequence of rings with
variations in thickness and other details can be recognized
in more than one tree, which means that any given line in a
tree can be correlated by comparison with a comparable
ring in another tree. The result of this is a time scale of
dendrochronology that can be extended further than the
lifetime of a single tree. Starting with a living tree for
which rings can be counted backward from the present,
characteristic patterns can be recognized in dead trees and
carried still further back in time. Living bristlecone pines
in California have given scientists a look at the past five
thousand years. When data are cross-correlated with dead
bristlecones, the record is extended to over nine thousand

years, a feat that is possible because the cold and dry climates where the ancient, living trees grow also retards the decomposition of dead members of the colony. Bald cypress trees are now being studied in lower Arkansas to yield information for the eastern United States. Individual cypress trees live as long as a thousand years —a long time but not up to bristlecone antiquity. However, dead cypress generally are quickly covered by swamp water and mud and thereby preserved from rotting just as effectively as in the cold, dry climate of eastern California. Thus, the cypress dates from living and fossil wood may extend tree-ring chronology in the Mississippi Valley to five thousand or more years from the present.

It goes without saying that scientists who count tree rings aren't just trying to beat a Guinness record for antiquity. The pattern of rings is indicative of past climates and other environmental factors. Episodes of storm, fire, disease, meteor impact, or insect attack are preserved in the wood, as are human artifacts like nails, carvings, and impact by sporty cars or musket balls. A forestry scientist recently studied tree rings near Mt. St. Helens and found that prehistoric eruption patterns were displayed in the old Douglas firs of the region. He suggests from his studies that there may be one or more large eruptions of St. Helens before the present activity lessens. We shall see if his prediction proves to be correct.

For all its usefulness, dendrochronology only gives information about the last ten thousand years at best. That may seem like a long time in human history, but it is almost trivial in terms of an Earth history of five billion years and more. However, tree rings, or even the lack thereof, do provide other sorts of information. To understand using trees beyond just counting rings, it is necessary to look more closely at the cause and timing of ring growth. The light and dark bands in a ring sequence are loosely called summer wood and winter wood, but those terms disguise the real situation. Studies have shown that the timing of growth of the wood is controlled by the length of day-light, the photoperiod, rather than a change in tempera-ture, water availability, or other factors. The photoperiod control presumably protects a tree from starting growth from the stimulus of a few early-spring warm days. At the other end of the annual cycle, the tree begins dormancy prior to harmful fall frosts or freezes. Response to photo-period rather than fleeting environment changes is clearly advantageous to the individual trees, and that behavior seemingly has been perpetuated during evolution.

Because photoperiod is the controlling factor, large trees growing near the equator show no growth rings or have very weakly developed ones, for the length of day is con-stant or nearly so throughout the year. The greater the dis-tance from the equator, the larger the contrast in day length with season and the more pronounced the rings. An addi-tional factor is that wood grows faster in warm climates than in cold.

Given these two observations, one can look at fossil wood as a guide to ancient climates. Plants that produced large, woody stems appeared in the Devonian Period (about four hundred million years ago) not long after land plants first appeared. No Devonian wood with rings has been found, but then all known Devonian fossil wood has been found in places that were near the equator at the time of their growth. This is not to say that the local-ities where the fossil wood was found are near the equator now, for the fossils were found in Indiana, New York, Russia, and Spitsbergen. One must remember that the continents have moved about quite a lot during earth history. Their past positions can be estimated by measuring the orientation of "fossil" magnetism in the rocks that was locked in at the time of their formation. By reading the magnetic information, one can infer that the wood localities were all within twenty degrees latitude of the equator four hundred million years ago.

In rocks of the Carboniferous Period (about 286 to 350

million years ago) there have been found a few specimens of wood that exhibit rings, but the period seems to have been one of warm climates, with rapid growth of mostly ringless wood, which conforms well with the paleolocation of the great coal swamps in an equatorial belt.

In rocks of the Permian Period (248–246 million years ago) there are ringless woods from a broad tropical belt, but there are also strongly ringed fossil woods found from localities that had higher Permian latitudes. Again, the pattern of ringed-wood distribution correlates well with other geologic evidence that tells of polar glaciations and a climate not unlike that in the more recent ice ages of some tens of thousands of years ago.

For the Mesozoic Era (248–65 million years ago), and here we are getting closer to the present, there is abundant geologic evidence that worldwide climates were very warm. The tree ring data fit this supposition well. There was a broad equatorial zone with trees that were ringless or with only faint rings. In high latitudes there were trees with well-developed rings, indicating a strong seasonality, but the rings are wide, indicating rapid growth from an equable climate.

At present, there are very few trees at high latitudes, indeed none at all beyond the Antarctic Circle, and those few northern ones show narrow growth rings indicative of the severe climate above the Arctic Circle. The amount of sunlight received at high latitudes during the growing season is more than enough, but the temperatures limit growth severely or prevent tree survival.

Thus, the evidence from fossil wood is in agreement with that from paleomagnetism and other geologic evidence with respect to both world climates and the distribution of the continents. Such confirmation of conclusions from more than one type of evidence constitutes a consensus of data that gives scientists confidence in their ideas. In other words, one might say that the interpretation of paleomagnetic data survives the test of tree-ring data.

The counting of tree rings is doubtless seminal to all other studies of growth lines, but the fact is that fossil wood is relatively rare when compared to other fossils as well as being relatively difficult to identify to a fine taxonomic subdivision. By contrast, remains of marine organisms with skeletons made of resistant materials such as calcium carbonate are both abundant and easily characterized.

Leonardo da Vinci recognized growth rings on the abundant fossils of Italy, but little study was done on such features for many centuries. Earth science is inevitably strongly tied to localities where rocks happen to be exposed, and thus it was that a surgeon named John Jeremiah Bigsby collected fossil Silurian corals during an expedition to the upper Great Lakes in the 1820s. He noted in a written report in 1824 that the corals showed structures that might indicate their age. Other workers studying modern corals came to similar conclusions over the next hundred years or so, culminating in studies by the Chinese biologist T. Y. H. Ma, who published papers in the 1930s attesting that corals in subtropical latitudes showed pronounced annual growth structures, whereas those from tropical habitats showed no growth rings and very rapid growth—shades of tree rings.

Ma's papers were published during the same time period that a young graduate student named John Wells was pursuing a doctorate at Cornell. Wells, who had an interest in the local corals of New York—corals like those seen by Bigsby over a century before—had suggested in a paper in 1937 that some lines between the presumed yearly expansions on some fossil corals might represent monthly fluctuations in growth. There are yet finer growth lines on corals, though, that many scientists, including Wells, suspected were perhaps daily growth features.

The fine lines were not preserved on most fossil corals, however, being easily worn away or covered by encrusting organisms, so their study was set aside in favor of other interests. Earth science progressed in various fields, and the question of the fine lines on corals became more meaningful, principally because of two seemingly unrelated developments.

One of these resulted from a combination of astronomy and geophysics wherein the question arose as to when the moon became associated with the earth. Part of this question revolved around the effect of lunar tides on the earth. A widely accepted theory was that the effect of tides on the earth was to gradually slow down the rotation of the earth as the moon moved ever so slightly farther away from the earth. This was a fine theory, and one that was generally accepted by astronomers, but there was no way to test it because neither that change in rotation nor the change in distance from the earth to the moon could be measured with sufficient accuracy over a short time. All one could wish for was some sort of a way to judge the number of days in a year in the geologic past and hence infer the rate of rotation of the earth.

During the same time peroid, the age of the earth was a topic of great interest. By the early part of the 1900s radioactivity was being used to date the time of formation of minerals, and by mid-century there were numerous methods being utilized in many laboratories.

Thus, an absolute age scale for the history of the earth was established, concurrent with a theory about the earth's rotation slowing down with time. The radiometric dating methods depended on a great many assumptions, none of which could be shown to be unequivocally true, and the rotation idea was pure theory, however widely accepted.

John Wells, then a professor at his alma mater, wrote about that condition of understanding in a 1966 paper:

> Can paleontology, a rather simple-minded science, provide anything in the way of verifying the pronouncements now emanating, at a very considerable expense, from the black boxes? Can paleontology give any support to the shaky chronometric creation of the geophysicists and astronomers?

Wells published the results of his study of coral growth lines in 1963 in the prestigious journal *Nature*. He had counted the fine lines between the presumably annual breaks on corals and found that the average for Devonian corals from New York was about four hundred. If the lines were daily growth lines, then the length of the Devonian day was shorter than at present, and the year had more days. That, of course, is exactly what one would expect if the rotation of the earth had been slowing down since some time in the distant past.

Since that time, Wells counted more corals' rings and found 412 rings per year from an Ordovician coral, 400 from a Silurian one, an average of 398 from some Devonian ones, 398 from a Mississippian one, and 380 and 390 from a couple of Pennsylvanian samples. It seems that simple-minded paleontology had confirmed "existing theories of paleogeophysics," to use Wells's words. S. M. Awramik and J. P. Vanyo of the University of California at Santa Barbara have recently reported daily growth features in the Precambrian algal fossils called stromatolites that lead to an estimate of 435 days in the late Proterozoic year, more than 600 million years ago, a figure that fits well with Wells's data. It is worth noting that the theory of the rotation of the earth slowing as the moon recedes has also been confirmed by accurate measurements of the rate of recession of the moon made by bouncing laser light off a reflector placed on the moon by some recent visitors from Earth.

It is unfortunate that growth rings on corals are so rarely preserved, because a fossil with daily rings dates itself on an absolute scale, not just in relation to other fossils. This is so because if one knows the number of days in a year, one also knows the age of the earth when that was the case. At present, the fine lines on a coral provide only a confirmation of other theories, but one wonders if further work might make it the standard rather than the handmaiden of geochronology—a coral clock as it were.

However poetic the concept of a coral clock, corals are

not as common as fossils as some other creatures, and attention has turned to the more common clam and other bivalves. Not only are specimens of bivalves easier to come by, but the growth is recorded by structures within the shell as well as on the surface, so loss of detail by abrasion, solution, or other surface modification is not as serious a hindrance as with corals.

As with many scientific endeavors, closer study reveals complexities undreamed of by previous workers. It's the old story of the more one knows about a subject, the more one recognizes what is unknown. With many bivalves, the annual growth lines are obvious on the outer part of the shell—so far, so good. However, when scientists began to count the finer divisions between the annual ones, they discovered that they were not simply daily but were related to some other set of external factors. The rhythm of shell deposition, like all biologic rhythms, is doubtless partly controlled by internal timing mechanisms in the organism, but those mechanisms are influenced or entrained by external clues.

To understand what external clues were important, scientists studied living bivalves. Some took the approach of placing bivalves in aquaria in the laboratory where conditions could be controlled. Laboratory experiments clearly have the advantage that the animals are always available for examination. The lab people found that light-dark cycles did act as clues, as might be expected. They found to their distress that examining the animals also triggered formation of growth lines in the shells. Thus, the more they studied their specimens, the more they perturbed the cycles—a disappointing business to say the least, especially for scientists who prefer to do their work indoors.

Others studied the animals in their natural environment. One approach was to tag bivalves, return them to their normal habitat, and then recover them later to see what growth had taken place. That proved to be a task that was easier conceived than consummated. One fisheries re-

searcher marked 41,000 specimens of an ocean quahog,
returned them to their natural habitat, and recovered a
paltry 60 a year later. Another scientist tagged 470 specimens of a Pacific clam, released them, and later recovered
none—a discouraging business.

Still, progress was made. Researchers showed that layering in bivalve shells is tied to tidal changes, local environmental changes, seasonal differences, storms, and a host
of factors. The effect of water temperature was demonstrated
by measuring the ratio of two isotopes of oxygen in mollusk
shells. It had been shown in the 1940s and early 1950s by
Harold Urey and others at the University of Chicago that
the relative abundance of ^{16}O, the common form of oxygen,
and ^{18}O, a less common isotope, in mollusk shells was
related to the temperature of the water in which the animal
was living. Sampling of layers in bivalve shells showed that
the annual change in environmental temperature was indeed recorded in the shell. Measuring the $^{18}O/^{16}O$ ratio
in shell material requires a great deal of painstaking sample
preparation as well as the use of elaborate and expensive
analytical techniques, but its use did serve to establish
that annual cycles are preserved in mollusk shells. Knowing
that, researchers could use the much simpler technique of
counting the annual growth increments.

A recent study by Douglas Jones has cleared up much
of the picture for bivalves. While a graduate student at
Princeton, Jones studied numerous specimens of commercially harvested clams from the Atlantic off of New
Jersey. His study has not only provided paleontologists and
biologists with valuable information, but it provided Jones
with a supplemental food source while a student, since his
live specimens were highly edible as well as scientifically
useful.

Jones studied specimens collected every two weeks for
two years and was thus able to trace the growth of shell
over the whole year. He found that the growth rings were
indeed annual but that they were related to the time of

spawning of the clams rather than to other factors such as temperature or other seasonal changes. He was able to recognize stage of growth of a shell in the context of the annual growth cycle. Recognition of growth stage is valuable because he then could determine when, in the seasonal growth cycle, a bivalve expired. That may seem of little use, but consider that the same determination could be made as well on fossil shells as with modern ones. In a fossile accumlation there is always the question of whether the assemblage of shells represents a group of animals that died all at once in a mass-mortality event or whether the shells accumulated over a long period from gradual dying off. Such a distinction is valuable to a paleontologist attempting to reconstruct past environments and past geologic history.

Having proved that the growth increments were annual, Jones made the somewhat astonishing discovery that bivalves are very long lived. Several common species of edible clams live several decades instead of the five or six years previously assumed by many. Even more amazing, the ocean quahog *Arctica islandica* seemingly routinely lives to a century or more. A Russian marine biologist found one bivalve specimen of another species that was 150 years old.

So it seems that bivalves preserve a lengthy record in their shells. They are no match for a bristlecone pine, but they may be the oldest living invertebrates and possibly the oldest living animals. One wonders if there might not be a quahog or two out in the Atlantic that was happily building shell when people landed at Plymouth rock. Also, if their life span is so long, it may well be that harvesting of edible bivalves is depleting the population more than one might have thought. It is sobering to realize, to quote Jones, that "to find some of the oldest animals known one need travel only as far as the soup section of the local grocery store."

Other workers have compared growth patterns of clam-like mollusks and their look-alikes, brachiopods, from different

growth environments and have found, as might be expected, that the same species shows different growth characteristics that reflect differences in its surroundings,
nutrition, and other factors. Thus, growth line studies can
be used to characterize ancient environments in terms of
conditions as well as giving information about age of the
deposits.

Vertebrates grow by stages just as do trees and bivalves,
and some of their skeletal parts can be utilized for the
information layered into them. In mammals the growth of
bone doesn't leave obvious layers or lines except with
teeth where layers of so-called cementum deposited on
the outer surfaces of horse teeth show some promise. With
fish, though, there are easily visible growth lines and layers
in parts of the skeleton. Scales, otoliths (an internal ear
bone), spines, opercular bones (the bony plate that covers
the gills), and vertebrae all show growth layers reflecting
seasonal changes. In temperate climates, growth of winter
bone is slower than summer bone, which leaves clearly
visible, dark, translucent bands from winter and chalky
white layers from summer. With freshwater fish in the
monsoon tropics, the onset of the dry season shows in a
manner similar to winter growth. There are also rings
formed from secondary causes, such as change in diet or
migration of the fish from salt to fresh water or vice versa.

As a graduate student, Mike Voorhies of the University
of Nebraska studied a remarkable fossil site near Orchard,
Nebraska, for his classic doctoral dissertation. He found
huge quantities of mammal remains which, because of their
age distribution and conditions of burial, he assumed had
died in a catastrophic event rather than just through
normal attrition. He was naturally curious about what the
time of year was when the mass burial took place. Mike
knew that fish vertebrae were supposed to show growth
features, and his fossils included some vertebrae of catfish.
Mike's father is an avid fisherman and was more than
happy to provide him with specimens of modern fish from

the area. The vertebrae showed the growth lines clearly with dark winter layers and light summer ones. When Mike's mammals died, though, the climate in Nebraska was somewhat more tropical than today, so he wanted to check some fish vertebrae from a less seasonal place. Fortunately, the late P. O. McGrew of the University of Wyoming had just returned from Florida, where he had studied death and burial of modern fish in a lake. He provided Mike with some crappie (*Poxomis*) vertebrae, and sure enough, although the bands were less obvious, they were still clearly visible. Mike checked his fossil catfish vertebrae and found that the fish had all died in winter. From that he concluded that it was highly probable that the mammals had died in a winter storm, possible with snow covering their food supply and stressing them with cold. Quite a bit of evidence from a fish bone.

There is an element of the public who imagine that scientists gather their data in spotless laboratories, or at the very least in careful field studies with little room for frivolity or casual acquisition of information. Yet there was Jones getting his tasty subjects from the Atlantic. And what about Voorhies? Well, he isn't much of a fisherman himself, but you can be sure that those modern fish his father supplied made a few tasty meals at the old farmhouse where he stayed while in the field. And McGrew told us many a scientific tidbit when he returned from Florida, but as I recall, the fishing stories outnumbered the scientific ones by a fair ratio. And anyway, why shouldn't research be edible? I'll have mine with a little parsley, lemon, and garlic butter—perhaps with a nice brisk white Pinot, asparagus, and some crusty bread.

CHAPTER SIX

Aqua Spectaculars and Other Disasters

When I was a youngster, Hollywood studios were continuing a phase of water movies that was started in the silent days by Mack Sennett's bathing beauties. There were the Tarzan movies with former Olympic swimmer Johnnie Weissmuller doing the crawl across jungle rivers and ponds, stopping here and there to wrestle a crocodile or avoid a fuming hippo. Then there were the costly, gaudy film versions of water ballets featuring symmetrical arangements of symmetrical girls in scanty and form-fitting one-piece bathing suits. These usually starred Esther Williams, whose well-muscled body always looked a bit out of place in street clothes in the infrequent scenes filmed out of a watery setting. Those grandiose productions gave way to beach movies with Bardot and other unusually shaped young women wearing a minimum of attire.

I gather from advertisements in newspapers that the beach movie survives to this day as an entertainment for teenagers whose scantily attired minds mesh well with the genre. We can breathe a sigh of relief that the aqua spectaculars' time seems to have passed forever, for they were the true disasters of the water movies. Granted, none of the water movies had much of a plot, but at least it is not unreasonable that a bunch of young people might spend a lot of time partying at the beach. There never was anything reasonable about the contrived happenstances that managed to provide Esther Williams with an orchestra and a corps of swimmers everywhere she went.

A few water movies even starred actors and actresses with all of their clothes on but featured watery disasters as an important element of the story, with hurricane-driven rains, giant waves, walls of water from burst dams, and other catastrophic events creating the central trial of a celluloid morality play by bringing out the best or worst in characters or eliminating the evil and saving the pure of heart.

Whether natural disasters have any moral effect on humans is questionable, but there is no doubt that catastrophic events that involve water are as widespread today as they were throughout geologic history. Many submarine earthquakes transfer part of their energy release to the ocean, with resulting tsunamis, often incorrectly called tidal waves, sweeping onshore with great destructive force. Heavy rains in mountains and deserts can send masses of water rushing down canyons or dry arroyos to sweep away houses, cars, and people.

Some natural water catastrophies result from water stored in a natural reservoir such as a lake. As any geologist will tell you, lakes are temporary features in the long term. Before you hurry to sell your Minnesota or Ontario cabin, be assured that in the time frame of geologists, a life span of a few hundred or thousand years is temporary. The fact is that lakes do become filled in with sediment and accumulated organic matter over periods of many years to form rich agricultural land in temperate climates, dry playas in desert regions, and unstable building foundations in Mexico City.

Some lakes change to nonlakes through catastrophic emptying rather than gradual infilling. A common natural sequence begins with a mass of weakly consolidated rock and soil sliding downhill to form a dam in a valley bottom. With the flow of the stream in the valley blocked by the slide mass, water backs up to form a lake behind the newly formed natural dam. Unless the dam is leaky, the water accumulates over a period of time. One of two results generally occurs. The water pressure behind the dam may build up to the point at which underground water movement into and under the dam causes it to weaken and burst. Alternately, and this seems to be the commoner of the two patterns, water eventually tops over the dam. Because the dam was formed from an incohesive body of rocks and soil, it is readily eroded by the running water, and the opening in the dam becomes quickly deepened and widened, which results in more water flow and more erosion in a rapidly increasing sequence of positive feedback that culminates in the dam washing out catastrophically.

A well-known example of a natural dam washout occurred in the Gros Ventre valley east of Jackson Hole, Wyoming. On June 23, 1925, a rain-loosened rock mass slid into the valley to form a dam over 200 feet high. Water accumulated behind the dam until May of the next year, when flow over the top began. Erosion rapidly lowered the opening by 50 feet, releasing 1.9 billion cubic feet of water down the valley. Blocks of rock 15 feet across were carried down the valley, and the village of Kelly, 4 miles down the valley, was swept away by a wall of water 15 feet high. A comparable disaster was prevented some four decades later when an earthquake at Hebgen Lake, Montana, caused a giant rockslide that damned a river. With prior knowledge of Gros Ventre and other slides, the omnipresent Corps of Engineers used heavy equipment to lower the dam and prevent a dangerous accumulation of water.

There have been other catastrophic releases of naturally dammed water in historical times in India and the Soviet Union, but for a truly vast dam washout we must look to the prehistoric past. Some time between fifteen thousand

and fourteen thousand years ago a giant flood event occurred in northern Utah when the precursor of Great Salt Lake, Lake Bonneville, partially washed out its dam. Studies show that the lake had risen steadily during the interval between twenty-six thousand and sixteen thousand year ago, after which the level stabilized at the level of Red Rock Pass, near Preston, Idaho, over which it drained to the north. Sometime later, downcutting of the soft sediments at Red Rock Pass accelerated, and Lake Bonneville's waters rushed down Marsh Creek Valley to join the Snake River at about the site of Pocatello, Idaho. A great flood followed approximately the course of the present Snake River, flooding broad valleys, depositing coarse debris, and enlarging narrow places in the river valley by massive erosional events. Near Rupert, Idaho, an area of 300 square miles was flooded to a depth of 50 feet. Near Homestead, Oregon, 500 miles downstream, the flood waters reached 290 feet above normal river level.

The great USGS geologist G. K. Gilbert discovered evidence of the Booneville Flood during his late-nineteenth-century study of ancient Lake Bonneville. While he summed the flood up as a "debacle," he did not have the opportunity to observe the effects of the immense discharge downstream from the Red Rock Pass region, and hence he underestimated the magnitude of the discharge, conservatively comparing it to the flow of the Niagara River. A more accurate estimate sets the peak flow at about 15 million cubic feet per second, or more than a third of a cubic mile per hour. That is three times the average discharge of the Amazon River.

Peak flow is thought to have continued for a few days or weeks and large volume discharge for at leats a year. Huge boulders were swept along and deposited on hillsides far above the normal river level. Somewhat less than half a cubic mile of bedrock was also removed and transported downstream. The coarse debris deposited by the Bonneville Flood is mostly an unlayered mixture of sand and coarser pieces up to many feet in diameter. Geologists studying the region in the early parts of this century thought that the large rounded boulders were just stream-worn, in-place blocks or boulders fallen from nearby lava dams, because they could not conceive of flowing water of such quantity and velocity as to actually transport such giant pieces of rock. Knowing what we now know about the great Bonneville Flood, it is no wonder that there are legends of ancient flooding in the traditions of the Indians of the Pacific Northwest. We will see later that the ancient Indians had more than the Bonneville Flood from which to construct a history of flooding in the region.

Certainly no one could argue that such floods are major disasters, but at least they happen only once. When the dam has washed out or a valley cut into it, there is longer a reservoir in which to store water for a future flood. In the context of the buffer concept, the buffer formed by the dam is destroyed during the energy release so that it cannot again store energy—in the form of water in these examples. The pattern is one of a rapidly increasing release of water (energy) to a peak value followed by gradual decline as the lake (buffer) empties to a stable level.

There are, and have been, natural lakes that dump over and over again, causing repeated flooding. Lakes behind beaver dams are a widespread example. The hardworking beavers generally keep their dams in good repair, but a heavy rain or wet season can get ahead of them and result in collapse of the dam and release of the water. Such floods are generally comparatively small, however, and can hardly be called catastrophies in the sense of the Lake Bonneville or even the Gros Ventre flood—except of course for the beavers, for whom it might be called a *Castor* disaster.

In Alaska and adjacent parts of Canada there are numerous lakes that fill, empty, and fill again in more or less regular successions. Flooding from these so called self-dumping lakes is sufficiently large to cause major damage to roads, pipelines, and human habitation, and there are many valleys that are "forbidden" in local Indian lore because of the now-and-then occurrence of a catastrophic flood. Similar floods occur in the Andes of South America as well as mountainous regions of Europe and Asia, and they are sufficiently common in Iceland to have been given a name—*jökulhlaup*—a glacier burst.

These strange lakes form when a mass of glacial ice dams a river. In the usual case a glacier from one valley dams a river in another at their junction. Glacier ice makes a fine dam because the buried ice is plastic under the weight of the overlying ice and forms a tight seal to the walls and floor of the valley. Water accumulates behind the ice dam to form a lake, the size of which depends on circumstances of topography.

In none of the ice-dammed lakes studied has the water level risen to the point at which water pours over the dam. Instead, leakage begins near the base of the dam. This is attributed to one or both of two effects. Deepening of the lake increases the water pressure at the bottom to the point at which the strength of the ice is exceeded and water forces its way through the base of the dam. In addition, since ice weighs less per unit volume than water, there is a buoyancy effect. As the water deepens, the ice dam tends to float off its base. Either or both of these factors allow a leak to start near the base of the ice dam. Enlarging of the outlet tunnel by melting effects of the moving water increases the flow in a positive-feedback cycle not unlike deepening of an overflow channel. In either case, the rate of flow starts slowly, increases rapidly to a peak, then tapers off over a period of time, just as with earth-dammed lakes.

In many instances, the dam is destroyed, and water, mud, and icebergs rush down the valley to wreak havoc below. In others, the lake drains out through the tunnel under the dam, and then the tunnel reseals itself by flowage of ice under the influence of the weight of the overlying glacier, in some instances before the lake is altogether emptied.

Like many periodic phenomena in nature, self-emptying lakes are not on a perfect time schedule. As a result, it's difficult for the geologist to be at the lake at the right time to observe the emptying. Such endeavors can be a frustrating experience. One team of researchers studied a lake in Yukon Territory, Canada. After a preliminary survey the year before, they returned to the lake in 1979 with state-of-the-art electronic equipment to monitor lake levels automatically all summer so that the emptying event could be documented in every minuscule detail. They arrived at the lake and began to prepare to deploy their elaborate equipment. Almost as if triggered by the scientists' activity, the lake began to empty, and the fancy instruments were cast aside as they were forced to run about the lake's receding edge, painting the time of day on emerging rocks as the only possible way of recording the rapidly falling lake level. To paraphrase Burns, the high-tech schemes o' mice and men gang aft a-gley.

Lake George in Alaska used to be highly predictable. According to local Indians, it had flooded about every fifteen or twenty years prior to the turn of the century. Starting in 1918, it began to empty on an annual basis. Beginning in 1935, the annual emptying began a little earlier each year and then missed 1963 when no ice dam formed. Lake George formed and emptied again in 1964 through 1966. In the case of Lake George, the breakout followed a predictable pattern, with seepage starting where the glacier pressed against a valley wall. Seepage increased until the ice broke down and a gorge formed through which flow was very rapid. It took about five days for maximum flow to occur after the beginning of seepage. Lake George was so regular that highway department crews, scientists, and tourists regularly reserved a week during late summer for the event.

Many scientists have attempted to understand the phenomenon of self-dumping lakes on a quantitative basis. Such an exercise is useful for prediction of flood as well as for the pure science of it. If a complicated mathematical model predicts the behavior of a natural phenomenon, then that lends support to the truth of the model. On the other hand, if a model fails the test of prediction, then it must be discarded or modified.

Thus it was that a geophysicist G. K. C. Clarke of the University of British Columbia refined the theoretical model of a previous worker (the Nye model) to arrive at a very elaborate framework of the behavior of ice-dammed, periodic outburst lakes. Using fifty-seven different variables, he made a prediction of the peak discharge from one outburst. The other extant model (the Clague-Mathews model) used only one variable. Predictions by either model were about equally good, to the dismay of the Canadian who wrote that the simpler model gave "an amazingly good prediction considering the formula depends only on reservoir volume and requires no prior knowledge of tunnel geometry and slope, Manning roughness, or the other variables that appear in the Nye model." He further wrote that "the relationship, if any, between the Clague-Mathews formula and Nye's model remains mysterious." One can be sympathetic to the geophysicist's discomfort, but one must always be ready to accept a simple explanation or relationship if it works. Adding more variables to a mathematical model of nature may only make the model longer and more complicated, not necessarily a better representation of nature. A variable is of no consequence if it has no effect on the outcome. It is a bit like picking the winner of a horse race by the color of the horse plus the color of the jockey's clothing plus the number of boards in the stall door, etc. One could make an elaborate handicapping system, but would it pick winners?

The principle, or maxim, that applies here, called Occam's (or Ockham's) razor, is that one should not add complications to an explanation of a phenomenon if they do not add to understanding. I have a feeling that William of Ockham, the fourteenth-century English philosopher

who espoused the principle, would have been fond of the
Clague-Mathews model.

Modern-day glacier-dammed lakes produce large floods
and provide grist for the mill of hydrologists, glaciologists,
geophysicists, and others in the earth-science fraternity, but
they are altogether trivial in magnitude when compared
to some outbursts that occurred in the past. I am not
referring to the great flood from ancient Lake Bonneville,
for in spite of its vastness and power, it, too, was minor
in comparison to a series of great floods that burst forth
from a lake in Montana and swept across Idaho and
Washington, stripping the land clean to bedrock and de-
stroying essentially everything in their path.

There is a vast region from Spokane, Washington, south-
westward to the Columbia River over which there are
numerous dry stream valleys, ridges of large boulders,
stripped rock surfaces, and other unusual features. During
the 1920s those so-called scablands were traversed and
examined by J Harlen Bretz of the University of Chicago.
(That's no mistake; Bretz's first name is just J with no
period.) Bretz saw clear evidence of the work of moving
water on a scale previously unimagined except by wild-
eyed catastrophists. Bretz, like his contemporaries, was
raised and trained in the gradualist tradition established
by Charles Lyell. According to Lyell's teaching, Bretz must
look to modern processes to explain what he saw in eastern
Washington, but Bretz's eyes and mind told him differently.
He imagined a flood of unthinkable magnitude that swept
the land clean, carved giant valleys into tough, resistant
basalt lavas, and transported huge masses of coarse sediments. He remained convinced of his theory in spite of its
rejection by his geologist peers, no small segment of whom
simply assumed that Bretz has lost his senses.

Bretz stuck by his ideas, and they gradually gained grudg-
ing support from some of his closest associates, though he
was still regarded as a nut by geologists at large, mostly
because he could produce no source for all the water re-

quired to perform the colossal amount of erosion his theory demanded. He proposed that the water came from melting of glaciers, but his critics insisted that there was no way to melt that much ice in a short enough time to account for a flood of the magnitude he suggested. He published papers on the subject throughout the 1920s expounding his unambiguous field evidence. Gradually, people began to accept his bizarre ideas, especially as other workers demonstrated that there was a source for the vast quantity of water required in glacial Lake Missoula.

There was abundant evidence in western Montana that there had once been a great lake covering much of the area. Study showed that a lobe of the last great glacier created a dam near the Idaho-Montana line east of present-day Pend Oreille Lake. The dam held back a lake that covered almost 3,000 square miles and contained more than 500 cubic miles of water—mighty Lake Missoula. In the Missoula, Montana, area the evidence is obvious. From the campus of the University of Montana one need only look to "M" Hill to see traces of ancient shorelines of Lake Missoula far up on the mountainside, traces that are especially obvious if a light dusting of snow has fallen and partly melted. Similar shorelines are found on many mountainsides in the region.

Bretz called upon Lake Missoula for a source of the water for his great flood. In the 1940s, USGS geologist J. D. Pardee had called attention to a number of features in western Montana that must have owed their origin to unusually large volumes of moving water, observations that fitted well with Bretz's ideas. By the 1950s most of Bretz's critics had become silent, and his theory was accepted, if grudgingly, by his contemporaries. He was later to receive the Penrose Medal of the Geological Society of America from the very group who refused to believe his youthful fancies.

Finally, almost everyone agreed that not only was Bretz right but that Lake Missoula had been emptied during a

catastrophic destruction of the ice dam which held back
the veritable inland sea. By comparison with modern ice-
dammed lakes, it was assumed that the ice dam either
leaked or was floated loose from its base by the waters of
the lake. That done, the ice dam collapsed, and a large
part of the 500 cubic miles of water rushed westward to
produce the scablands. In some places small lake basins
were carved out of solid bedrock by the rushing water, and
giant ripple marks were left downstream from obstructions.
The ripple marks were so large that they were difficult to
recognize except from an airplane, but they were unequivocally ripple marks. Bretz had walked up and down
them without realizing that they were there.

Geologists also noticed that there were layered deposits of
finer sediments left by the waters where they had slowed
enough to deposit their suspended load. It was postulated
that some mechanism caused the draining of Lake Missoula
to proceed in pulses rather than a single great flood, although nobody could come up with a reasonable mechanism that might explain this. Some assumed that there
might have been two or more emptyings controlled by
long-term climatic fluctuations during the last ice age.

Then a radical suggestion was made, in the grand tradition of Bretz, that Lake Missoula hadn't emptied just
once or even several times but about forty times. R. B.
Waitt, Jr., of the USGS published his ideas in the same
journal that Bretz had used, *Journal of Geology*, published
at the University of Chicago. Waitt has shown that there
are some forty floods recorded in the rhythmically layered
lake sediments found in western Montana. Some argued
that the layers represented pulses in a single flood, but
Waitt was able to show that the tops of layers were broken
and disturbed by overlying deposits, a feature that could
only occur if the top of the first layer had dried and
become consolidated by long exposure to the air before the
second one was deposited. Furthermore, there are earth-
filled rodent burrows in the tops of layers that must have

been dug in the past during intervals between floods, for they are now much too far below the surface to be of recent origin.

Using a combination of radiocarbon dating of enclosed fossils and volcanic ash layers and some assumptions about the rate of water accumulation in Lake Missoula, Waitt proposed that about thirty to fifty years elapsed between successive floods. The whole package of evidence suggests that Missoula existed, with periodic emptying, for about two thousand years between fifteen thousand and thirteen thousand years ago.

The timing means that the Bonneville Flood occurred during the same interval as the Lake Missoula emptyings. The relations have not been worked out to everyone's satisfaction, but there is no doubt that the Bonneville Flood deposits are sandwiched between those of floods from Lake Missoula.

The total amount of water per flood may not have been greatly different for the Bonneville Flood than for the many floods from Lake Missoula, but the *rate* of water release was very different. In one place the flowing water was a mile wide, a thousand feet deep, and flowing at about 45 to 60 miles per hour. To put those numbers in perspective, that means a flow of about two hundred times that of the Mississippi in the flood stage. Put another way, the flow during the maximum hours of a Lake Missoula glacier burst was more than that for all the rivers of the world. That's a flood.

As I mentioned before, there are legends of a great flood in the lore of the Indians of the region. Before we jump to the conclusion that their ancestors remember the floods and that they recounted them over campfires in an oral history since the times of Lake Missoula, we must remember that there are no completely credible records of man in North America prior to about twelve thousand years ago. It is more likely that the first Americans saw the result of the floods and drew their own conclusions just as a modern

geologist would. After all, if the origin of the landscape in
eastern Washington was plain to Bretz after thirteen thousand years, it certainly should have been obvious to a
new immigrant from Asia after only a thousand years.
The astute Indian geomorphologist also would have had
the advantage of never hearing about Charles Lyell and
uniformitarianism, so he could believe his own eyes without
the scholarly baggage that even Bretz carried. You might
say that the evidence of the floods was the stuff that legends
were made of.

CHAPTER SEVEN

Journey to the Center of the Earth

My father has often expressed puzzlement that people go to bars and cafés after work and sit around laughing and talking animatedly when there are so many serious social and political problems to be solved. That has never puzzled me, because I just take it as a fact of life that most people don't give a hoot about serious issues—social, political, or otherwise. What has always seemed a bit strange to me is that a high proportion of people don't really seem to care about the nature of the world around them. It appears that there is a substantial segment of mankind made up of people who just are not curious about much of anything. I belong to that segment at the opposite end of the scale made up of people who are basically just nosy—perhaps inquisitive is a more tasteful euphemism.

Curiosity can take a lot of forms. Someone with a small sphere of interest might take pleasure in eavesdropping on a neighbor's conversations, peeking through the window to see who's coming and going, and maybe sneaking a look at the postcards in the apartment mailbox and the empties that find their way to the trash bins. Those of a scientific inclination can bird-watch, study insects or trees, or start a mineral and fossil collection.

On a grander scale, a person might read gossip columns and magazines or enjoy taking trips to meet new people and see new things or become interested in the politics of distant countries or the wildflowers of another continent. Ease of travel and communication has considerably broadened the horizons of such explorers in the past couple of centuries. In days past there were adventures of exploration available for the willing. My teenaged son is envious of those explorers, for his wish is to map an unknown corner of the earth—on foot.

In past millenia explorers of variable talent and veracity visited far-flung parts of the world to bring home charts and tales of wonder and even to plant their country's flag on unclaimed real estate. It didn't take long for travelers to ascertain that the earth wasn't flat or perched on the back of a giant turtle or made up of several levels inhabited by different sorts of humans and humanlike gods. Even with general agreement that the world was more or less spherical, the whole story was unknown. The atmosphere could be studied from the ground and later from balloons and other aircraft, but the mystery beneath the feet was still profound.

Man had lived in caves for millenia, so had some knowledge of what lay under the earth at shallow depths, but there fact ended, and speculation took over. There were legends of gnomes and dwarfs whose occupation was mining and who lived in vast networks of tunnels beneath mysterious mountains. Some imagined that the earth was hollow, with a different race living in the interior.

Persistent beliefs grew up in many cultures about an underworld ruled by nasty gods where conditions were highly undesirable. In some versions there were pools of boiling oil or molten brimstone (sulfur) where those who had offended the gods when above ground were given endless and unthinkable punishment.

False rumors about the surface of the earth could be

struck down by exploration of remote places, but the wild ideas about what went on below the ground weren't subject to such easy testing. There were deep water wells and mines but little else to go on. Indeed, deep mines were hot, and there were volcanoes around the Mediterranean and in Iceland, and around the volcanoes there were places where sulfurous gases spewed forth. People had seen tunnels in lava flows. Were those tunnels entrances to the underworld?

In Jules Verne's *Journey to the Center of the Earth*, Professor Lidinbrook of Hamburg discovers an old Nordic parchment that tells how to enter the crater of the volcano Sneffels Yokul in Iceland and thereby visit the center of the earth. The professor and his party do just that and after wild adventures finally emerge safely from another volcano in Italy. Verne wrote pure fiction, of course, but the idea of worldwide volcanic plumbing was not purely from *his* imagination. Ignorance was vast a century ago, and such a scenario was not wholly unacceptable to many.

Information was slowly gathered. Water wells gave a peek at the first few hundred meters, but coal mines went even deeper. The search for metals, especially precious metals, carried man's look still deeper, with modern mines going down to 3,000 meters (10,000 feet). It was the search for petroleum and natural gas that gave scientists the first really deep probes into the crust, with depths of 5,000 to 7,000 meters (16,000 to 23,000 feet). The deepest petroleum exploration well as of 1984 was one in Oklahoma called the Bertha Rogers well, which was bottomed at 9,974 meters (33,000 feet, or over 6 miles). Drilling was stopped at that depth because molten sulfur was encountered, a fact that might give pause to some who pooh-pooh the idea of an inferno with brimstone pools or ammunition to a fire-breathing preacher warning of the dangers of not being saved.

The deepest drill hole is in the USSR on the Kola Peninsula near the border with arctic Norway. As of 1984, it was deeper than 12,000 meters (39,000 feet) with a goal of

around 15,000 meters. The Kola well hasn't encountered
any brimstone, but it did pierce a zone that contained
abundant flowing, hot water at 4,500 meters (15,000 feet)
just as Professor Lidinbrook's guide, Hans, found in a deep
volcanic tunnel. The Soviets plan a number of additional
deep drill holes at various places in the USSR, but it is
unlikely that any of them will be appreciably deeper than
the Kola hole. Technical problems of drilling so deeply will
doubtless always limit direct looks at any but the first few
miles of earth's skin.

Another way to look beneath the surface of the earth is to
listen to vibrations transmitted through the rocks. Earthquakes provide naturally generated sounds that are affected
in various ways—bent, reflected, or not transmitted at all—
by the rocks they pass through. From seismological studies of
earthquakes, scientists have made some inferences about
the deep structure of the earth, but only in the broadest
terms. Seismologists have also used artificially generated
sounds from explosives to examine sound-transmission characteristics of rocks up to a few miles deep, especially in
petroleum exploration. During the last couple of decades,
exploration seismology has become more sophisticated.
Computer processing of data yields fuzzy pictures of the
arrangement of subsurface rocks, though it reveals little
about their detailed makeup. Such information is limited
to depths about the same as deep drill holes.

Thus, our journeys to the center of the earth are limited
to about the top 0.15 percent of the whole distance to the
center, a far cry from Professor Lidinbrook's goal. We know,
or think we know, from earthquake seismology that the
earth is built of concentric shells of differing density and
that the temperature increases downward, but we know
precious little else. There are a few places where rocks from
the upper mantle are exposed, and we do find chunks of
mantle rock carried to the surface in lavas, but that is about
it. We are reasonably sure that the crust under the oceans is
about 5 to 10 kilometers (3 to 6 miles) thick and that under

the continents about 30 to 100 kilometers (20 to 60 miles) thick. Seismic data have been interpreted to indicate that the continental crust is composed of an upper part made of granitic rocks and a lower part made of basaltic rocks like the oceanic crust. Under the continents there is a seismic break called the Conrad discontinuity that was originally assumed to be the granite-basalt change. The Kola drill hole has shown that it is a boundary, at least there, between fractured rock with fluids in the fractures and dry, solid rock. The change between the crust and the mantle is placed at another seismic break called the Mohorivičić discontinuity, where it is thought that basalts give way to more dense rocks of a different mineralogy and chemical composition.

While most earth scientists accept that broad picture, there is no direct proof of most of the concept and no way to test it. We have seismic data, gravity data, magnetic data, and other geophysical measurements, but the raw data must be interpreted and a model developed that stands until new data render it obsolete. Most of the earth is inaccessible and will probably always be, yet the curious want to know more about it. How can we learn more? We can try to simulate the deep earth in laboratories by studying rock and mineral samples under conditions of high temperature and pressure like those deep in the earth.

The first earth scientist who is known to have conducted laboratory experiments to simulate the formation of natural rocks was Sir James Hall, who in 1798 published a paper in the *Transactions of the Royal Society of Edinburgh* describing the melting and cooling of basalts from Scotland and Italy. He found that rapid cooling of the melts resulted in a glass, whereas slower cooling produced a crystalline rock that closely resembled the original basalts. Hall was a supporter of James Hutton and a loyal plutonist who wanted to prove the igneous origin of basalts by his experiments. (Plutonists, who thought that rocks such as granite and basalt formed by crystallization from melts, opposed

the Neptunists who attributed their origin to precipitation
from seawater.) Hall's basalt melting was done at atmospheric pressure, so it cannot really be counted as a look
within the crust, but it was a first step in experimental
petrology, the laboratory study of the origin of rocks. Hall
is reputed to have heated some ground marble confined in
a plugged gun barrel to simulate both high temperature and
high pressure. In this experiment it is a wonder that he
wasn't killed or at least injured inasmuch as very high
pressures of carbon dioxide were doubtless generated within
the gun barrel, high enough to burst it with great violence.
Apparently Hall had good gun barrels, good luck, or both.
He did conclude, erroneously as it turned out, that calcium
carbonate was injected as veins into rock from a melt rather
than deposited from water passing through open fractures.
It should be stated that Hall was using his experiments to
counter the views of opponents of Hutton who believed
that granite veins were deposited from water, so he was
predisposed to interpret the "marble" veins incorrectly.

Experimental petrology grew slowly, with various scientists using observations on the behavior of slags formed in
smelting processes to explain features observed in igneous
rocks, mostly drawing conclusions of dubious merit. In
1910 a young man named Norman L. Bowen came to the
Geophysical Laboratory of the Carnegie Institution of
Washington to do a series of experiments that were to form
the basis for a doctoral dissertation at M.I.T. Bowen was
trained as a geologist but also understood the importance
of applying principles of chemical thermodynamics to his
geologic studies. For forty years Bowen continued with the
Geophysical Lab (or Gee Whiz Lab as some wags call it),
studying many types of igneous rocks in his crucibles and
furnaces. Like Hall, Bowen mostly studied melting of
silicates at atmospheric pressure, but he carried his studies
far beyond simple melting and cooling of whole rocks. He
prepared simplified mineral mixtures that allowed him to
control variables closely, drew wide-ranging conclusions

that were to influence several generations of geologists, and set experimental petrology on a solid base. Later in his career he would study the melting of granitelike mixtures in the presence of water under pressure, as would be the case deep in the crust. The journey was begun.

Five years before Bowen left Cambridge for Washington, D.C., another graduate student across town at Harvard was studying materials under high pressure. P. W. Bridgman was a pioneer in every sense of the word, not only was he the first person to study a huge number of elements and compounds under high pressure, but he also designed all of his own equipment. It would be altogether correct to say that Bridgman invented the whole field of high-pressure research. In those days it was almost as difficult to study materials under high pressure in the laboratory as to study them in the earth itself. The problem is severalfold.

In the first place, it goes without saying that the material studied must be confined under high pressure. That means there must be a source of the force that generates the pressure and there must be a vessel to contain the specimen. A source of the force is relatively accessible, for all one needs is what amounts to a very large hydraulic jack with a frame to allow the force of the piston to be applied to a specimen container. The container must have a space for the specimen and be made in such a way that it won't leak and won't rupture from the great pressures inside of it. That is easily said and less easily engineered.

What sort of pressures must be generated and contained? For a pressure unit we will use 1 atmosphere, the pressure of the earth's atmosphere at sea level, which is about 15 pounds per square inch, or about 1 kilogram per square centimeter. A few pressure values will help give a sense of magnitude. The pressure inside the cylinder of a high-compression auto engine is about 10 atmospheres, that in a scuba tank is a little over 100 atmospheres, and that at the bottom of the deepest part of the ocean about 1,000 atmospheres. Readers who are old enough may recall the

spherical vessels used for undersea exploration half a century
ago. They were cast of thick steel, with very thick windows
to resist pressures far less than 1,000 atmospheres. For geologists, however, the desired experimental pressures might
start at about 100,000 atmospheres, equivalent to that at
the top of the outer mantle. As it happens, 100,000 atmospheres was the highest pressure attained by Bridgman in
over a half century of experiments. Really high pressures
are difficult to attain.

Another factor that is overlooked by nonspecialists is that
it is difficult to measure conditions such as pressure or
temperature in the specimen vessels. One might think that
all that would have to be done is to measure the force of
the hydraulic ram and divide that by the area of the pressure cell on which that force was exerted. Alas, that might
work at a few thousand atmospheres, but at meaningfully
high pressures, friction and other resistance within the pressure cell are so very high that a calculated pressure would
be much higher than the pressure actually attained within
the cell.

Bridgman and others devised other means to measure
pressure. One way was to measure electrical resistance
through a wire in the pressure chamber. Another was to
use materials that undergo structural changes at known
pressures to give spot checks on a continuous measurement
such as electrical resistance. There is a bit of a Catch-22
angle here in that any pressure-measuring scheme must be
calibrated in a high-pressure vessel, which is of course where
we are trying to measure the pressure in the first place.

As if such difficulties weren't enough, consider that Bridgman had no way of directly observing what was happening
inside the pressure vessel. He had invented an extreme-
pressure cell early in his career that used tungsten carbide
anvils to squeeze a sample surrounded by a soft, ductile
gasket material. He discovered that no matter how much
force was applied to the anvils, there was no leakage from
the sample chamber, because the pressure in the gasket

material was always higher than that on the sample. Thus, he had a secure chamber but no way to look at it. Tungsten carbide is very hard and very strong, but it is as opaque as a piece of steel.

High pressures are also obtainable for a short time with the use of explosives. Charges of high-velocity explosives can be shaped in such a way as to concentrate their force over relatively small regions. Such shaped charges are the basis for armor-piercing projectiles but can also be used in the laboratory. Conditions of temperature and pressure deep within the earth can be simulated for a very brief interval. Explosives are even used for commercial production of synthetic diamonds.

Various sorts of pressure devices were contrived by other researchers, including some that used four hydraulic rams that all pushed on a sample that was tetrahedral in shape (a four-sided figure with sides that are equilateral triangles). Such devices attained high pressures on larger samples than in Bridgman's cells and were used to produce diamonds and other materials. Meanwhile, scientists at the National Bureau of Standards, University of Chicago, and at the Geophysical Laboratory began to devise high-pressure devices that used diamond anvils instead of tungsten carbide. Diamond is the hardest substance known, is strong under compressive stress, and best of all, is transparent to both light and X rays.

The present state of the art for high-pressure systems is a device about the size of a small book. Force is applied to diamond anvils by turning a hand screw that moves a lever against a piston. Samples are sealed inside a chamber that is just a hole drilled in a sheet of steel. The diamond anvils press on each side of the hole in the sheet, and the steel acts as a gasket while also forming the walls of the chamber. This simple Bridgman-type device attains pressures of almost 2 million atmospheres, which simulates pressures at 3,000 kilometers (1,800 miles) within the earth, about the boundary between the mantle and core.

The diamond cell allows the sample to be visually observed at high pressures, and X-ray diffraction can be employed to study the crystal structure of materials, as well. Lasers are used to heat the sample to desired temperatures so that both the high pressure and high temperature of deep subterranean environments can be simulated. Pressure is easily determined. A ruby fragment in the cell is illuminated by an external light. The ruby fluoresces with red light of a wavelength that is proportional to pressure. The diamond cell promises to provide important new data that can be used to increase the understanding of our planet's interior as well as those of other planets.

Still, in spite of the attractiveness of the diamond-anvil cell, it doesn't satisfy all the wishes of an experimental petrologist. An essential problem is that the size of the sample in a diamond-anvil cell must be very small, usually a small piece of a pure substance. Rocks are made up of many minerals and also include fluids such as water and carbon dioxide as part of their makeup. A petrologist would like to know about the melting and crystallization behavior of real rocks over a wide range of pressures and temperatures. If such information is available, then natural rocks act as geothermometers and geobarometers that tell the petrologist about conditions of formation of the rocks.

Many experiments have been performed using simplified rock systems under high pressure and temperature conditions simulating crustal environments. Such experiments have allowed geologists to make reasonable estimates of the temperatures and pressures of such processes as metamorphism, emplacement of granite melts, and the formation of ore deposits. Recent experiments have melted mantlelike rocks at very high pressures to produce unusual melts with chemical compositions like those of the igneous rocks found only in very old rocks, confirming ideas that conditions were very different in the early history of the earth.

Most natural rock systems, especially those in the crust, contain water and carbon dioxide as well as various solid mineral substances. In order to study such "wet" mixtures, experimental petrologists use strong metal containers that can be placed into furnaces and heated. The containers have the unsettling name of bombs, and many do rupture with considerable violence during experiments. Such conditions are called hydrothermal (hot water) and simulate most crustal processes. Many useful studies have given geologists important insights, but their application is limited to fairly low pressures. One clever person manufactures emeralds in hydrothermal bombs by a secret process. The so-called Chatham emeralds, after the person who makes them, sell for more than most natural emeralds.

Laboratory experiments at high pressures and temperatures haven't been confined to just squeezing and melting rocks. Structural geologists are interested in how rocks fold, fracture, and flow. To study such properties, the rock samples have to be held at appropriate conditions of temperature and confining pressure and then subjected to squeezing, twisting, or some other deforming force. The apparatus that allows rocks to be squeezed or bent is necessarily more complicated than the elegantly simple diamond cells. One consequence of that fact is that temperatures and confining pressures must be limited to those pertaining to the upper part of the crust, but that is the region of most interest to structural geologists in any case.

Experimentally deformed rocks have added greatly to our understanding of how rocks are able to deform plastically, without fracturing, but there are still difficulties facing the experimentally oriented structural geologist. Some materials, such as rock salt or marble, deform readily under laboratory conditions, but others, such as common sandstone, are less cooperative. The problem factor is time.

One can simulate crustal temperatures and pressures, but simulating the rate of change in either is another story. In the real world a layer of sandstone may be bent and folded into wild contortions without fracturing, but the bending and folding may have taken place over the course of ten

thousand years or more. Simulating such incredibly slow
changes in shape is just plain impossible. We can learn a
great deal from experimental deformation of rocks, but we
cannot imitate the building of the Alps or the Himalayas.
We simply don't have the time.

Some scientists have made scale models of rock masses,
using modeling clay, wax, tar, plastics, and the like to try
to defeat the time problem. They argue that they have
scaled everything in such a way as to simulate in a few
hours or days a mountain-building event that took a few
million years. To be sure, they have produced structures
that resemble the flexures and planes of slippage of the
earth's great mountains, but scaling everything is seemingly impossible. Real rocks seem to behave in a framework of the immensity of geologic time almost as viscous
liquids do in hours or days.

If scientists cannot imitate nature in the laboratory, how,
then, can they make a voyage to the center of the earth? One
way is to use the experimental data and develop theoretical
models. One needn't melt a piece of rock if there is a testable theory that can predict how that rock will melt. One
cannot set up an experiment to bend a slab of sandstone
over a period of ten thousand years. Even the most liberal
granting agency would want a report sooner than that. One
can bend the sandstone in a computer if the properties of
rocks are well enough known from a combination of theory
and experiment.

What we can do is visit the center of the earth and all
the places along the way in our minds. We can imagine
what it must be like based on fundamental properties of
minerals, rocks, and fluids that we know from measurements and infer from extrapolation. Within the confines of
our perception of how matter behaves, we can predict what
a trip to the center would show us. As the basic data of
earth science accumulates, is tested, and either verified or
thrown away, our visualization of the real earth will improve. Our scenario will be an improvement over that of

Jules Verne by the extent to which our knowledge exceeds that which was available to him. Our minds will take us to places that caves and drill holes will never go if we gather the knowledge to let us understand that last frontier beneath our feet.

CHAPTER EIGHT

Scat Song

Like so many English words, scat has a number of meanings. Some people think of it as a word to expel a cat from someplace where it is unwelcome, perhaps derived as a contraction of an expletive such as ssh cat! or scoot cat! or the like. Residents of the Shetlands or Orkneys know that scat is rent or tax paid to the government for land, from the Danish word with the same meaning. Jazz lovers recognize scat as multisyllable nonsense sounds sung in a silly imitation of a musical instrument. The origin of the scat in scat singing is debatable, but my guess is that it might have come about by a musician describing the singing to his colleagues: "Man, that's just scat." If that foray into totally unsupported etymology has any merit, it is because it would be a legitimate use of another meaning of scat—feces or dung.

It is this last meaning that I wish to pursue by a venture into the serious scientific field of scatology, also known as coprology. Scatology should bear no relation to scatological humor, but alas, scientists are people, too, and the science of scat automatically inspires chuckles from most people. An organized listing of fossil scat samples becomes a scata-

log, and so it goes. Perhaps because of the humorous under-
current, no scientist has seen fit to specialize wholly
in the study of fossil dung lest he or she become famous
in an unwelcome way. However, a great many scientists,
principally paleontologists, marine biologists, and archaeologists have made brief forays into the study of both modern and ancient scat.

Coprolites, the proper name for fossil scat, are fossils
just as much as are shells, bones, or tracks of extinct animals and in some instances provide information that is not
available in another way. Coprolites can give clues about
an animal's diet, its life environment, its locomotion, structure of internal parts, heredity, possibly its height, and
some have said, its origin.

Often people express surprise that coprolites are found
at all, but really the reverse would be more surprising. Consider that disposing of scat is an organism's way of disposing of comparatively large amounts of toxic wastes that
would be injurious if retained in its immediate environment. Production of coprolites seems to be unique to the
animal kingdom. Higher plants have limited capacity for
disposing of metabolic by-products and dissolved minerals,
so such substances are often incorporated into the structure
of the plant. Lower plants such as bacteria produce a
variety of by-products that accumulate in their growth environment, in some cases producing toxicity in a host animal
or plant, in other cases causing reduced growth and even
death of the bacteria themselves. A well-known example is
fermentation of sugars, as in the making of wine, in which
accumulated ethanol eventually reaches high enough levels
to kill off the yeast that produced it.

Animals avoid close-by accumulations of scat in a variety
of ways in nature. One strategy is for the animal to deposit
the scat and then leave—a simple technique if there is
somewhere to go that is not already contaminated. The
technique works fine for mammals, reptiles, birds, fish, and
many other mobile creatures. Scat from gastropods (snails

and their kin) is deposited periodically as the animal moves, leaving a characteristic trail that can be followed in ancient as well as modern settings without the special talents of an Indian tracker or bloodhound. Except in highly confined situations such as caves or small islands, normal decay of the scat acts to remove it or at least detoxify it.

Also, there are legions of organisms that are coprophagous—scat eaters. Coprophags produce their own feces, of course, which are in turn consumed by coprophags farther down the scat food chain until a tail-end coprophag must obtain the very last trace of nutrition and leaves a sort of terminal turd—an object stripped of all nutrients. The scenario may not actually occur, for more often than not the scat is broken down into various products that are dissolved and washed away or fragmented beyond recognition and incorporated into soil through the action of earthworms and soil microorganisms without formation of well-formed scat bodies.

Organisms that live out their lives in one place, such as mussels, barnacles, or corals, or those of limited mobility, such as burrowing clams or boring worms, cannot leave the scene to escape from their own excrement. As a result, they have developed strategies for disposal of their waste products. Some have life habitats in which water motion sweeps away the feces, the common mussel is a good example. It lives firmly attached to a rock in a high-energy environment of rising and falling tides and cleansing wave motion. Mussel excrement is produced in rounded pellets that roll readily, which makes them easily transportable away from the mussels' living space. There are thick modern deposits of mussel scat offshore from colonies of the ubiquitous bivalves. Other marine animals that live out their lives in quiet water use other techniques. Some of them expel their scat encased in mucous membranes along with a few gas bubbles for buoyancy, which causes the scat to float away from the animal's home ground. A species of sea urchin, those spine-covered, apple-sized relatives of the starfish, solves its disposal problem in a curious way. Sea urchins have their feeding part underneath and an excretory organ up among the spines. Thus, one can imagine a problem of the scat accumulating as a mass caught by the spines. It doesn't happen because there is a chemical substance in the excrement that causes the spine-erecting muscles in the skin to relax. Thus, the spines sag down, and the scat rolls down the spines and free of the urchin. Many burrowing animals solve the problem by digging dead-end tunnels and stuffing their droppings into them, plugging the entry with sediment—sort of a sanitary landfill.

I suppose a true coprologist could go on with examples almost forever, but I, like other scientists, wish to avoid that label, so I'll stop with those few examples and return to the question of why we find coprolites at all in the fossil record. The answer is tied into why we find fossils of any kind. In the case of whole organisms it depends on the dead animal, or usually its hard parts, such as shell or bone, escaping destruction by weathering or carrion eaters before it becomes buried in a place that allows for preservation. With coprolites, preservation is the real issue, because any given organism produces many times its body weight in excrement over a lifetime, so there is no shortage of original product, but the forces acting to destroy a scat before safe burial are legion. Even a scat that becomes buried is still subject to the effects of burrowing creatures and a milieu of scat-destroying microorganisms.

In spite of the forces acting to destroy scat, many coprolites are found and have been found for many years. The first scientist who made an issue of coprolites was the English geologist William Buckland. Buckland was a churchman by training who became reader in geology and mineralogy and later professor at Oxford in the early part of the nineteenth century. Reverend Buckland collected and studied some objects from the Jurassic rocks of England that had been interpreted elsewhere as fossil evergreen cones. Buckland correctly reinterpreted them as coprolites.

He found fragments of various animals in the coprolites and thought that they were fossil scat from the great swimming ichthyosaurs. Modern specialists disagree with the ichthyosaur origin, but Buckland deserves a great deal of credit for his recognition of the fossils for what they were. Buckland's driving idea in his studies was to demonstrate the evidence for God's creation as found in the rocks. He studied coprolites from several ages of rocks and found that the shape of the objects was very much the same. He concluded that the similarity in shape showed that different animals had the same sort of excretory organs, which, in turn, proved that there was a divine design that was used over and over again in successive acts of creation. His observations were correct, although many would interpret them as favoring evolution rather than creation.

Not all churchmen approved of Reverend Buckland's ideas about coprolites as evidenced by comments in *A Brief and Complete Refutation of the Anti-Scriptural Theory of the Geologists*, written by an anoymous clergyman of the Church of England and published in 1853 by Werthem and Macintosh in London. He wrote:

> The geological assertion that the Creator of this world formed it in some parts of coprolites savours very much of Satan or Beelzebub, the god of dung. Geologists could scarcely have made a more unfortunate self-refuting assertion than this.

Buckland became known as a leader in coprology, and specimens were sent to him from many parts of the world for study, but the science of scat attained little importance overall. One difficulty that persists to this day is identifying the animal that dropped the scat. The coprolite can be examined microscopically and fragments identified that give clues to the diet of the animal that produced it, just as Buckland found remains of fish and juvenile ichthyosaurs in his original coprolites. Such a finding only shows that the animal was carnivorous and leaves the identification open.

Such is still the case today, although many attempts have been made to finger the producer of coprolites. Often there is an association of coprolites with vertebrate fossils, but the strategy of mobile animals is to deposit their coprolites in some place other than their immediate environment, so that association is probably misleading rather than helpful. Many scientists have used the size of coprolites to guess at their producer. When the late Paul Edwards was a graduate student at the University of Nebraska, he studied numerous coprolites from the Oligocene (40 to 25 million years ago) rocks of the White River badlands. The White River rocks are filled with abundant coprolites, much more so than older or younger rocks in the area. Edwards's problem was twofold. First, why were the coprolites so abundant, and second, what animal or animals left them?

The first question is one of reconstructing past conditions, a primary goal of any earth scientist in some sense or other. Edwards studied the coprolites by a variety of means and concluded that they were the fossil scat of carnivores. Studies of modern scat have shown that carnivore turds disintegrate much more rapidly than those of herbivores. Thus, Paul knew that the conditions must have favored rapid burial of the scat—before forces of disintegration could crumble it. The Coprolites were confined mostly to fine-grained, clay-rich layers in the rocks rather than those composed of water-washed sand. Edwards interpreted the fine-grained layers to be accumulations of rapidly deposited volcanic ash that quickly buried the coprolites and ensured their preservation as fossils. One could argue that such an interpretation could have been made without the coprolites, but the White River rocks had been misinterpreted by many previous workers, so the fossil scat did contribute to their understanding.

As to the previous owner of the scat, that was up for grabs. Edwards measured a large number of coprolites and found that they fell into three crude size groups. He also measured skull size of the major carnivores known by their fossils from the White River rocks. There was a grouping into small, medium, and large, but beyond that, there was no way to positively attribute a given-sized coprolite to any particular Oligocene mammal.

I was told a story by the late Paul McGrew when he and I were colleagues at the University of Wyoming. It seems that a paleontologist studying coprolites was concerned with assigning the coprolites to the mammals who produced them. As one test he manufactured synthetic coprolites of the same size as his fossils and tried to duplicate the consistency as well as he could by comparing them with modern feces. His real coprolites had bent-over ends as if from hitting the ground after falling, so he dropped the soft pseudoturds from various heights to ascertain the height of the extinct creature's anus and thereby identify the paleodropper. I have asked a number of Paul's students and colleagues, and we all think we know who did the experiments, but we're not sure. Our suspect is now dead, but it doesn't seem right to blemish his memory, so I'll leave our guess unwritten. As far as we know, the study was never published.

Size was also used in an attempt to explain a large spiral- or helical-shaped object found in Queensland, Australia, in the early 1930s. This coil of sand was over 2 meters (7 feet) long, and it was suggested that it could be a coprolite from a 15-meter-long (50 feet) dinosaur that was known to have lived in that area when the rocks containing the object were deposited. A 2-meter coprolite would certainly be a medal-winning piece of dung, but it is probable that the fossil is a burrow filling rather than a spectacular scat. There are similar, though smaller, helical burrows dug by lungfish.

In the southwestern deserts of the United States there are cave deposits that contain coprolites of large size that can only have come from giant ground sloths (*Nothrotheriops*) which inhabited the region prior to their extinction at the end of the last great ice age, about ten thousand years ago. The sloths used the caves for shelter, and layers of droppings accumulated over a period exceeding thirty-five thousand years. Even though the sloths were strictly herbivores, their scat is preserved without noticeable alteration of the original material because of the dryness of the cave environment. The scat of terrestrial herbivores is mechanically more resistant to destruction than that of carnivores but is highly susceptible to rapid decay. There is a report by W. S. Strain of the University of Texas at El Paso of bovid (cowlike animals) coprolites strongly resembling modern "cow pies" from the White River rocks where rapid burial à la Paul Edwards allowed preservation, but that is unusual.

The ground-sloth scat is so well preserved that it has been used for a variety of purposes. In some caves the sloths were resident over many generations for long periods, living atop their dried manure pack. There the successive layers of droppings can be dated by radiocarbon methods to put the whole deposit in a known time framework. Also, pollen grains extracted from the layers help scientists to make educated guesses about the climate during that time past. In addition, a careful sorting of the scat allows paleontologists to determine the diet of the sloths in some detail. One study shows that the relative abundance of the sloths' food plants changed with time and perhaps contributed to its demise as the fraction of a shrub called Mormon tea (*Ephedra*) increased. Mormon tea contains a fairly potent narcotic substance, so the poor sloths may well have disappeared from a natural drug overdose.

Alas, the part of the record in the most informative cave, Rampart Cave in Nevada, informative because of the completeness of the dung record, was destroyed by fire during the summer of 1976, although a portion was spared. Unlike many coprolites, the sloth accumulations were unfossilized and just as burnable as a pack of dried manure in a barn.

The size championship for coprolites will have to be awarded to some mammoth droppings found in a cave in Utah. Bechan Cave is a shallow, domed-roofed opening in the Navajo sandstone that is floored by what the scientists called a dung blanket. (Inasmuch as the residents slept on it, I'd think that a dung mattress would be more appropriate if we are to retain the bed analogy.) In the mass of dung, some 255 cubic meters (9,000 cubic feet) of it—and that's a lot of you-know-what—they found two unbroken coprolites about 24 centimeters (9 inches) in diameter. These world-class coprolites were attributed to mammoths because, like the giant horse apples that they resemble, they contain lots of fragments of grass. The coprolites of the giant sloth, who shared the region with mammoths, contain twigs rather than grass.

Other coprolites have been positively correlated with a single species. Deposits of droppings in caves can be attributed to bat species whose fossil skeletons are found in the fecal mass. Likewise, bird fossils in the guano accumulations on many small islands indicate the avians responsible for the mess. Vertebrate paleontologist Glenn Jepsen attributed some coprolites from North Dakota that showed deails such as sphincter pinching, grooving, gas holes, and impressions of twigs and rocks from their first resting places to carnivorous crocodiles. One assumes that they show no signs of having been dropped from a height, which would fit with crocodiles.

Ground sloths and mammoths are not the only animals that bed down on their own excrement. Horses will do the same thing. Both sloths and horses have fairly inefficient digestive systems, and their droppings are mostly undigested vegetable fragments, so the toxicity is low. I can attest to the comfort afforded by horse droppings, having put sleeping bags on such accumulations in high mountain areas where a fecal mattress as fine as that of the Utah mammoths built up where fishermen tied their mounts—to provide me the only alternative to bare rock.

Other vertebrates reside on top of their own droppings, or at least their leavings, and in so doing create extensive accumulations of fossils. Carnivores carry their prey to caves and consume them at their leisure. While they do go outside to defecate in most instances, the bones accumulate in the cave. Many bone deposits of value to paleontologists owe their origin to a carnivore's rubbish pile.

Similar accumulations are found in other environments. Some carnivorous fish subsist on shelled mollusks which they ingest whole and then crush with strong teeth. They go foraging and then return to home areas to digest their prey and defecate and by so doing create accumulations of the indigestible parts, for the broken shells pass through the fish unaffected to provide material for shell beds where the fish rest. The fish apparently lack acids in their digestive juices, for the shell fragments show no sign of solution. My former colleague at Wyoming, Don Boyd, has described mollusk-shell accumulations in rocks in Wyoming that are accompanied by teeth of the shell-crushing fish who presumably ate the contents. Shellfish-eating birds produce similar deposits, although the fragments are rounded by abrasion in the gizzard. Such deposits of rounded shell fragments would likely be misinterpreted as having resulted from water transportation because of the rounding. Some of the bird-laid deposits are from regurgitated material rather than feces, but the end result is the same. Many shell and bone layers in the geologic record may well be remnants of layers of feces from fish, birds, and other animals.

Even human coprolites have been found, mostly in caves. It seems that many a prehistoric cave dweller was reluctant to venture outside under some conditions and simply used a corner of the cave. That procedure doesn't sound like the best of housekeeping, but perhaps we shouldn't criticize. If it was a choice between the back cranny of the cave or going out in the dark to face a hungry bear or saber-toothed cat, you or I might have done the same thing.

At any rate, archaeologists have figured out tricks to disaggregate the human coprolites and examine them for indications of diet. For the former denizens of Mesa Verde,

Colorado, they have found what one would have expected: traces of beans, peppers, squash, cactus fruit, gourds, ground cherries, and a smattering of other plants. The ancient Mesa Verdeans seemingly ate very little meat. Similar findings have been made in Mexico with corn, tomatoes, and tomatillos added. It would appear that diets have changed little in the past thousands of years. Human coprolites have been recovered from sites in Europe, as well, and are under study for clues to the dietary habits of our ancient precursors.

Researchers with a medical bent have found remains of pinworms and tapeworms in the fossil feces, tracing human parasites back to our origins. One group at the Veterans Administration Medical Center in Salt Lake City has even attempted to characterize odors extracted from fossils of human feces as a guide to diet. It seems that rehydrated fossils of human feces have an odor indistinguishable from fresh, modern feces. A publication from the study lists the diet of a human subject who ate, drank, and chewed a variety of items over a four-month period in 1982 and whose feces were subjected to instrumental odor analysis. The subject ingested a remarkable variety of substances; one might say a startling list to come from Mormon country, including numerous alcoholic beverages, coffee, and snuff, some of which were detected in the gas from the stool samples. Beer was the only alcoholic beverage detected from the feces, so use of the analysis by law enforcement agencies to detect drinking drivers would seem to offer little promise. The detection of food items in his fecal vapors required a fancy instrument called a gas chromatograph with the discerning nose of a researcher at an instrumental orifice to identify what the instrument was sensing. An odorgram, as they call their results, of a human coprolite from Glen Canyon on the Colorado River revealed odors of burnt corn, meat, and licorice. Another from Hogup Cave, Utah, had fragrances of green leaves, grass, and licorice. The authors attribute the licorice odors to native wild licorice or another licorice-tasting plant of the region. The licorice smell was also reported a number of times in the odorgrams of their modern, human subject, although licorice didn't appear in his dietary list. He did eat Italian sausage once, so maybe the fennel seed did it, although the licorice odor must remain suspect in the world of odorgrams.

The researchers did note that human feces, fossil or fresh, could be distinguished from those of other species by the fact that they smelled worse. For coprologists without elaborate analytical equipment, I suppose a rule of thumb could be that if it stinks, it's human. The potential for comments that might offend a reader is so great that I will drop the subject before temptation overcomes my will to resist, although critics of V.A. hospitals might be tempted to leap on this bit of odor exploration as an example of the waste of taxpayers' money. I can see the headline now — "V.A. Researchers Sniff Past Gas."

As with so many things in the world, the magnitude of effects and artifacts from higher animals is almost trivial when compared to those from the so-called lower part of the animal kingdom. Vertebrates certainly have contributed their droppings to the rocks since their appearance on earth, but it is the mollusks, crustaceans, worms, and the like that have created vast accumulations of feces.

Scientists many years ago recognized the droppings of worms and other burrowers in many sedimentary layers, but they failed to appreciate fully the magnitude of some fecal deposits. Geologists found layers made of pellets of sediment and eventually made the connection that the pellets were coprolites. Once having concluded that, they realized that there were pellet layers of many sorts through-out the geologic column. As it happens, there are many creatures that make their living by eating mud, extracting a trace of nutrition and expelling vast numbers of tiny turds. Their scat consists of mud, as it must, and mud pellets are particularly resistant to breakdown. Many, and in some places, most, shale layers in sedimentary rocks were probably originally accumulations of fecal pellets.

Some fecal pellets are specialized in their chemical composition. Arthropods make their skeletons out of chitin, the material of fingernails and innumerable animals make arthropods their major diet item. The chitin skeletal material is comparatively unaffected by digestion, and the feces of these arthropod eaters are mostly the substance.

Still other creatures, including tiny arthropods, many mollusks, fish, and other aquatic forms, consume microscopic plants as their diet. Pellets from those creatures form thick layers. Wilmot Bradley of the USGS, a coprophile of long standing, has suggested that the vast deposits of oil shale in Colorado, Utah, and Wyoming originated as accumulations of fecal pellet layers derived from tiny shrimplike creatures that lived in the ancient lakes of the region. It has also been suggested that the source of much of the world's petroleum may be fecal pellets from small herbivorous organisms.

There is a huge deposit, about three billion tons, of the calcium-phosphate mineral apatite in the Kola Peninsula of the USSR. That is a remarkable amount of phosphates without parallel, because it is in association with igneous rocks rather than with sedimentary ones. Igneous rocks commonly contain traces of apatite, but seldom in any significant concentration. Bertram R. S. Mannheim, who lists his affiliation as the Institute for Applied Scientomania in Berlin, has suggested in a paper published in the *Journal of Irreproducible Results* (vol. 25, pp. 6–7, 1979) that the Kola deposit is the result of the impact of a one-mile-diameter, extraterrestrial coprolite mass. With the current interest in impacts by cosmic bodies, perhaps we should examine this concept more closely—or perhaps not. Mannheim's proposed extraterrestrial body would be identical in composition to what some earth scientists suggest that some extraterrestrial impacting bodies hypotheses are composed of.

Coprolites also have very practical uses for applied earth scientists. One of the important activities that geologists, particularly petroleum geologists, engage in is correlation, determining that a layer of rock in one place is the equivalent, on some basis, of another layer somewhere else. For that purpose, fossils are often used, and in some situations coprolites are the fossils. Coprolites of distinctive character are found in rock layers in a number of parts of Europe. In spite of the fact that the depositor of the original scat is altogether a mystery, the distinctive coprolites still provide a ready means of recognizing the special layers, as they have since the beginnings of geology.

Some coprolites are highly distinctive in shape and have even been assigned names and classifications. All this in spite of the fact that their source is unknown. Feces from vertebrates tend to be irregular or cigar shaped, with no remarkable surface features. In contrast, the feces of some snails, many small arthropods, and probably those from other forms are extruded through openings that impart a characteristic shape to them or carry internal structures that result from the imprint of internal parts of the digestive tract. These coprolites are useful stratigraphic indicators. They have the merit of small size, as well, which means that they can be found in small drill cores or chips of rock from drilled wells, which increases their utility greatly.

Thus, the science of scat has more applications in earth sciences than one might think. Just as a biologist can look at a modern dropping and tell quite a bit about the animal that left it, so can a paleontologist do the same with a coprolite. Geologists can study the nature of ancient environments by the state and style of preservation of coprolites, and oil-company stratigraphers can relate one subsurface layer to another by using microscopic ridges and grooves on tiny fecal pellets.

Coprology is not without its problems, however, and I'll close with a quotation from a letter that the great American

vertebrate paleontologist Al Romer, Agassiz professor at
Harvard, wrote to G. C. Amstutz of the University of
Heidelberg:

> By way of anecdote, a number of years ago I was told about
> an old lady in one of the little Texas towns who had col-
> lected curios of all sorts, including fossils. I went to see her
> and spent a pleasant lunch with her. In her collection she
> had a number of coprolites, which she thought were fossil
> grasshoppers. I tried to explain to her that they weren't
> grasshoppers. Well, what were they? Coprolites meant nothing
> to her and some other technical terms which I used did not
> get across. Both of us, I am sure, had in common an ordinary
> Anglo-Saxon word which explained the matter perfectly, but
> one could not very well use it at her dinner table. I finally
> got the idea across, and then told her a place where she could
> probably collect a quart or two. However, by then she had
> lost interest.

CHAPTER NINE

When Vulcan Speaks

People—as individuals and in groups as large as tribes or whole nations—have been frightened by volcanoes for as long as anyone cares to think about. It is only fair to allow that these people have many good reasons for their fear. Volcanoes are literally openings to the underworld, the underworld that bypasses differences in upbringing or beliefs, because volcanic eruptions are independent of belief. They are very real. Lava pours, deep-red hot, over the land; or clouds of screamingly hot, frothy pumice rush down slopes at a frightening pace, or shadowy volumes of fine-grained debris fall from the air to choke out life. Volcanoes are not a religious issue.

The earth is a roughly spherical object made up of layers. We all live on the outermost layer, the crust, which is made up of firm, crystalline rocks. The crust is about 5 to 100 kilometers (3 to 60 miles) thick, depending on where it is measured, and is, as the name crust implies, wrapped around a softer interior. The material beneath the crust is called the mantle, and there is general agreement that it is made up of rock that contains a bit more iron and magnesium and somewhat less silicon and alkalies (sodium and potassium mostly) than the crust. The mantle is also a great deal hotter than the crust, and at least the upper part of it is in a constant state of mixing and over-turning because of its need to rid itself of the heat gener-ated by the decay of the small amount of radioactive elements it contains. Part of this heat is released to the surface in the form of volcanic activity.

One can imagine that in an ideally simple earth the heat from radioactive decay would be released uniformly over the surface and radiated into space, but such is not the case. In the real world there is more heat moving about in some places than in others. Where a great deal of heat is trans-ferred up from the depths, we surface dwellers will find evidence in the form of hot springs, geysers, or even vol-canoes. Most hot-spring and geyser regions are the result of near-surface volcanism, but the great volcanic centers them-selves, in turn, owe their activity to goings-on in those unplumbed depths.

Because the heat from the interior of the earth doesn't reach the outer layers uniformly, earth scientists speak of hot spots, places where mantle heat exits from the interior more aggressively than at other locations. Why the hot spots are where they are is a question of great interest, but we needn't be concerned about that question here. The fact of the matter is that heat from the interior of the earth flows more freely in some places than in others. Where there is heat there can be volcanic activity.

Even in the absence of hot spots, rocks can become hot, even melted, by being moved downward to hotter levels in the earth. That sort of movement takes place at the active edges of some continental masses when rocks from one slab of crust are shoved under the edge of another in a process called subduction. Those rocks from the outer skin of the earth are placed into new conditions, where they melt readily, from a combination of increased temper-ature with depth and frictional heat from the movement of the plates, to form magma, which is able to rise into the overlying crust. Subduction is a slow process, and the time for old crust to become melted takes on the order of millions, or the low tens of millions, of years.

But back to hot spots for the moment. The whole idea of the localization of volcanism at hot spots, and the hot-spot theory itself, was proposed by J. Tuzo Wilson of the University of Toronto from the example where the theory is best illustrated: the Hawaiian Islands. The islands, which are all of volcanic origin, are arrayed in a line with active volcanoes at one end and seemingly dead, older-looking ones at the other. This obvious difference in appearance of the Hawaiian chain is confirmed by radiometric dating as well as native legends; in fact, the islands were formed serially from the oldest one at the northwest end of the chain to the presently active ones at the southeast end. Wilson's explanation of this was that a great slab of crust, a plate, moved slowly over a heat source and the volcanoes formed over the hot spot as the plate moved on its journey.

Wilson's idea was a good one and is widely accepted today by many, if not all, earth scientists as a working hypothesis. Earth scientists use the hot-spot theory as a daily tool and speak of plumes in the mantle that bring up heat by convection of sticky mantle material rising hot and falling cooler like so much oatmeal on a temperate wood stove. And, befitting the comforting wood-stove analogy, the eruptions from such hot-spot volcanism are generally the less frightening ones to most of us.

Hawaiian volcanoes erupt on a fairly regular basis, and in spite of their televisible fountains of red-hot lava and the now-and-then overrunning of a housing development or school, they are really pretty well behaved volcanoes. Hawaiian eruptions are not very explosive, and there is ample time for authorities to move people and animals out of the way of the activity. Hawaiian volcanoes are slow, maybe even respectable.

It is probably not really quite fair to call Hawaiian volcanoes slow, because the kind of lava that flows from Kilauea is a relatively fluid type called basalt. It is the sort of material that makes up the crust beneath the oceans. As lava goes, basalt is a high-speed type. Because of its relatively low viscosity, basalt is able to flow over low slopes for great distances. Thus, basaltic lavas can form vast plains such as those we find preserved in southern Idaho and parts of western Oregon and Washington, where fluid lavas flowed out to form vast lakes of melted and hardening rock in the not so distant past. Similiar events took place in Siberia and India in the past several hundred million years, and there is ample evidence of such great floods of basalt flowing out onto the earth's surface almost from its beginning. However, as much as such outpourings must have affected the face of the land and the creatures that lived on it, they were events that took some time to happen. Days, weeks, perhaps even longer, passed while even a single flow moved out, quieted, and cooled. The great flows of basalt were not violent in the sense of a tornado or a tidal wave or a truly destructive volcanic event. The big events are not those of flows or emission of steam but of violent explosions and flying rocks and catastrophe.

The difference between the slow, quiet destruction of plantations, schools, and dwellings in Hawaii and the violent disruption of land and life over hundreds or thousands of square kilometers is not so much one of a difference in energy released but a matter of the rate at which that energy is released at the surface of the earth.

There are two principal properties of magma, the molten rock beneath the surface, that determine whether an eruption is violent or relatively passive. Both properties relate to the chemical composition of the magma. An important variable is the amount of gas, principally water, dissolved in the magma. The gases in a magma body are dissolved only because the entire mass is under considerable confining pressure by virtue of both the weight of overlying rock and additional pressure provided by forces within the crust. As the magma rises to shallower and shallower levels in the crust, the dissolved gas starts to come out of solution in the lower-pressure environment. If the gas evolves slowly, it may reach the surface to form a gas vent, usually redolent of sulfur compounds, hydrochloric acid, and all manner of noxious vapors. If, on the other hand, the magma moves fairly rapidly toward the surface, the gases evolve from the hot rock much faster, often resulting in explosions or formation of frothy masses of liquid rock.

The other chemical property of the magma that influences the violence of an eruption is its content of major elements, especially silicon, iron, magnesium, and the alkalies. In a molten rock silicon is linked together with oxygens to form long chains and irregular frameworks like the child's toys that use dowels to link wooden hubs. In melted rocks the silicons and oxygens are like a Tinker Toy construction, with every other hub a different color, a very irregular framework, as if made by a child with no sense of order. The alkalies are stuck into the holes in the framework and are linked to extra bonds on the silicons.

Such a structure in a liquid makes the liquid very viscous, because the silicon-oxygen linkages are strong and not easily broken; in effect, they hold the liquid together. Ordinary commercially made glass has such a structure, and if you have ever watched a glass blower, you will appreciate the fact that silicate glasses are viscous indeed.

If a magma contains appreciable magnesium and iron, those elements also form links with oxygen, but their chemical properties are such that they cannot link oxygens to other oxygens. Each iron or magnesium acts to terminate the oxygen chains, as if one used Tinker Toy hubs with only one hole in them. Thus, the more iron and magnesium in a molten silicate, the less linkage between atoms and the lower the viscosity of the liquid.

Basalt, the type of volcanic rock that usually erupts in a

stately, even quiet manner, contains relatively large amounts of iron and magnesium, so it is comparatively fluid. The volcanologist turned geophysicist, John Verhoogen of Berkeley, observed an antelope overtaken by a basaltic flow moving down the flank of an African volcano, and speeds of up to 30 miles an hour have been reported at various places. Because of their low viscosity, basalts also tend to release dissolved gases easily, accounting for their modest eruptive behavior.

The iron- and magnesium-poor magmas not only don't flow readily, but they are so sticky that gases cannot escape readily. The strength of the viscous glass holds the gases back until it escapes violently, often with spectacular results.

A comparison might be made with a bottle of a carbonated beverage left unstoppered. The dissolved carbon dioxide gas evolves slowly, and the drink goes flat. In contrast, in a bread dough, the carbon dioxide produced by fermentation is trapped in a viscous material, and the dough expands. If a bread dough is allowed to expand too long before baking, a large bubble will form in the dough, and the top of the loaf will collapse when the gas finally escapes. In an oven, that just ruins the loaf. In a volcanic eruption it might ruin a whole region.

Basalt outpourings are mostly fairly quiet, but ofttimes enough dissolved gas is trapped to form a furnace-clinkerlike material made of basalt filled with gas bubbles to create a rock formed like a sponge. Volcanic cones built up of such material dot the landscape of the western United States and Mexico, and geologic relations tell us that many of them were formed in the past few thousands of years. Obviously they must have been observed by native Americans; in fact, at such a cinder cone in California, I found a broken Indian pot with the volcanic bomb that broke it still sitting where it fell.

That pot was probably broken about eight thousand years ago, but as recently as the 1940s a crack opened in a cornfield in Mexico. The farmer kept filling it with earth, but it grew, and gases started to issue from it. In short order a new basalt vocano, Paricutin, as born. It is reasonable to expect more such volcanoes to form in future decades.

Some basalt volcanoes are not as short-lived as cinder cones but can still be fairly nonviolent. The island of Stromboli, between Sicily and Italy, is a volcano that has been erupting for centuries but has never had a really violent eruption. It is more violent than a Hawaiian volcano, but not much. It belches forth sticky blobs of lava on a periodic, though irregular, basis, often every few minutes. The explosions of lava are accompanied by noisy bursts of gases. Clearly, dissolved gas at Stromboli doesn't have the opportunity to accumulate to dangerous levels because it is constantly being expelled in small amounts. In fact, Stromboli is a good example of a highly active volcano that is apparently quite safe to live on. There are villages within a half mile of the summit and crops raised all around.

With more viscous magmas, the picture is quite different, and all of the great destructive eruptions arise from such sticky masses. Great eruptions consist of one or more of a number of disastrous events, and no one eruption exhibits all of them. There is the explosive release of gas, outpouring of lava ejecta with resulting ash falls, downslope movement of clouds of hot gas and ejecta, mudslides, and even destructive waves of water.

Almost all volcanic eruptions are preceded by indications that one would think would warn volcanophobic persons to beware, but the warnings are commonly ignored. For one thing, dangerous volcanoes are the so-called inactive ones. That may sound like a curious statement, for many people interpret inactive to mean dead, but such need not be the case. Mt. St. Helens was considered to be a volcano that had stopped erupting. Inactive volcanoes are, in many cases, volcanoes that are storing energy since their last eruption, getting ready for another one. It would be interesting to compare insurance rates for properties near a volcano like Mt. Etna on Sicily, which erupts almost continuously, with a similar property on the side of Mt. Hood or Mt. Rainier in the Pacific Northwest. Hood and Rainer show little or no sign of activity. Are they safer than Mt. Etna? From an insurer's point of view, perhaps Hood and Rainier are safe because there is little likelihood of their erupting during the term of a five-year policy, but the geologic risk is great—on a long-term basis.

For example, R. L. Christiansen of the USGS has shown the giant eruptions at Yellowstone Park have taken place at 2.0, 1.3, and 0.6 million years before the present. The interval between eruptions is 700,000 years. This appears to be a textbook case of a buffer system, and we can reasonably expect the next eruption to happen in about 100,000 years. Is Yellowstone dead? To the insurance actuary yes, but I'll consider it active with a long buffer-filling period.

The principal early warning signs from volcanoes are earthquakes caused by the ascent of magma from the depths. With a network of seismographs to pinpoint the location and depth of quakes, seismologists and volcanologists might notice an ascending series of tremors and be in a position to predict an eruption. One difficulty is that explosive volcanoes generally occur along the margins of continents where oceanic crust is in the process of being subducted under continental crust, and earthquakes are common in such regions, anyway, so many early warnings go unnoticed. The upward movement of magma also causes the sides of a volcano to swell almost imperceptibly, but every volcano would have to be instrumented or directly observed to detect such signs, a procedure that is just not possible in a world with thousands of possibly dangerous volcanoes.

In spite of these difficulties, it should be possible to anticipate when a volcano will erupt with a great violence, because volcanoes don't just "awake" with a giant, destructive roar; they awake slowly, as do most of us. After local earthquakes and possible swelling of the ground, activity may begin at a summit crater or other orifice with gas emissions or even minor explosive activity. Over the course of weeks or even months, activity ceases, then starts again, with a general tendency for more violent activity with each episode of renewal. Eruptions may last longer, and multiple vents may become active. Violent eruptions may occur, giving the appearance of the final event, but who can judge which is the final event? In the case of great eruptions, the final events occur as the individual eruptions become more and more closely spaced and more and more violent. The last, greatest event generally destroys the volcano, and activity declines fairly rapidly with a few after-eruptions.

For example, the volcano Tambora in Indonesia erupted in what is considered to be the largest explosive event in history. It is thought that the volcano had been inactive for about five thousand years before the 1815 eruption—plenty of time to store energy for a big outburst. Tambora began to be moderately active for at least a year prior to the main eruption with quakes and volcanic activity. Then, on April 6, 1815, activity increased, with expulsion of airborne debris and explosions heard 1,400 kilometers (900 miles) away. Intermittent activity continued until April 10, when a really violent eruption commenced, with columns of flame rising in the air to great heights. Ash falls and flows and collapse of part of the volcano followed. A sea wave was generated that caused extensive damage. Intense activity continued for about twenty-four hours during which explosions were heard 2,400 kilometers (1,400 miles) away. It is estimated that a total of 175 cubic kilometers (38 cubic miles) of ash was ejected in the whole eruption.

One of the most famous eruptions in history was that of Krakatau (also called Krakatoa) in 1883. Like Tambora,

Krakatau was located in Indonesia, but it was located in
a busy shipping lane between Java and Sumatra, so observations of the full course of the activity were considerably more detailed. The Krakatau eruption was to
come from a group of uninhabited islands of which Krakatau was the largest. It consisted of a line of volcanic cones,
the southernmost and largest of which was called Rakata
in Javanese, which got twisted around to Krakatau in the
Dutch-English jargon. There were reports that there had
been a big eruption there in 1680–81, but no details were
known.

There were no reported eruptions from any of the islands
during the interval, and it is likely that none occurred,
because the ship traffic past them was fairly heavy, and
such matters are recorded in ships' logs.

The Krakatau eruption sequence is a classic example of
the lengthy process that leads up to a major eruption, with
a gradual, though irregular, increase in activity as the main
event approaches. In the late 1870s frequent minor earthquakes began in the region, with a big one in 1880 felt
as far away as Australia. Like almost all volcanic regions,
however, earthquakes were a common event and no relation
to volcanism was suspected. The quakes increased in violence until May 20, 1883, when Krakatau began erupting,
with explosions heard 150 kilometers (90 miles) away, followed by an outpouring of steam and ash. Activity quieted
down by May 27, when a party visited the island and found
that the northernmost cone of the island was the source
of the activity and that it was continuously blowing out
steam, ash, and some lava.

Activity tapered off, seeming to some as if it were
going to stop altogether, but then, on June 19, the ash
column grew higher, and eruptions began in earnest, now
coming from two openings. That activity gradually increased, and by August 11 a visiting Dutch government
surveyor reported that from his vantage point on a boat

he could see three major eruptive centers and a number of minor ones. Activity continued, leading up to the climatic events of August 26–27. The only surviving eyewitnesses who were close by were on boats, because the violence of the eruptions generated sea waves that killed most of the coastal dwellers on nearby Java and Sumatra.

A Dutch geologist, R. D. Verbeek, pieced together information from many sources, including more than fifty ships' log books, and has given a fairly complete picture of the spectacular events of those two days. By 1:00 P.M. of August 26, explosions were heard 150 kilometers (90 miles) away, and the cloud was estimated to be 25 kilometers (15 miles) high. By 3:00 P.M. that day the sounds were heard 240 kilometers (140 miles) away, and by 5:00 P.M. were so loud that residents of Batavia, 160 kilometers (100 miles) away, described it as similar to close-by artillery fire.

Unbelievable as it may seem, during all of these eruptions a ship, the *Charles Bal*, tacked in little zigs and zags within 20 kilometers (12 miles) of the volcanoes, having been trapped there by unfavorable winds and darkness. The ash fall was so thick that the captain couldn't see to get away and was forced to remain close to navigate by the red glow of the eruption.

On the morning of August 27, activity appeared to be quieting down, but that was just a pause before the *real* events. Later in the morning, at 5:30, 6:44, 10:02, and 10:52, there was a series of explosions without parallel in historical records. The greatest one occurred at 10:02 and was heard in South Australia, 3,224 kilometers (1,930 miles) to the south and at Diego Garcia Island in the Indian Ocean, 3,647 kilometers (2,190 miles) to the west. The great sea waves were generated at that time, killing 36,000 people. In Batavia windows were blown in and buildings damaged.

Meanwhile, vast quantities of ash were being thrown

into the air, and some reached Batavia, though most fell into the sea. The hapless *Charles Bal* and another ship, the *Sir Robert Sale*, were sailing around in almost total darkness while their crews shoveled ash off the decks and out of the sails. The log of the *Sir Robert Sale* indicated that bombs as large as pumpkins were falling on the deck.

At 7:00 P.M. another violent series of explosions took place, and activity again increased until 11:00 P.M. when it began to diminish. At 2:30 P.M. on August 28 there was one final, small exposion, and quiet returned to the Straits of Sunda. Verbeek estimated that 15 cubic kilometers (3 cubic miles) of ash had been thrown out. Most of Krakatau had been destroyed, along with a neighboring island, though two nearby islands were actually larger because of accumulation of ash. Miraculously both the *Charles Bal* and *Sir Robert Sale* survived more or less intact.

Different volcanoes follow different courses and cause different sorts of geologic effects. Some eruptions, such as that at Vesuvius in A.D. 79, which buried Herculaneum in mud, or the 1985 eruption of Nevado del Ria in Colombia, which buried a village in mud, don't do their damage by explosions but by rainfall and melting snow accompanying the eruption, softening old and new ash accumulations, which then move rapidly downslope. Such mudflows off of volcanoes are common in Indonesia and the Philippines, as well. Others, like that of Mt. Pelée in Martinique in 1902, send glowing clouds of white hot ash and gas racing down slopes at speeds that would easily overtake a highway patrol car.

The great sideways blast of Mt. St. Helens in 1980 gave the clue to geologists that such dry avalanches are commonly present around similar volcanoes, and numerous of the ancient horizontal landslides have been recognized in many regions, especially around the North Pacific.

Some volcanoes never seem to become violent, spending their energy gradually without it ever building up to catastrophic proportions. In addition, some magmas simply don't contain enough gases to generate the explosive activity that characterize great eruptions. Many eruptions, including some late events at Mt. St. Helens, begin with slow movement of a mass of viscous lava to form what is called a dome. Often, dome building precedes a violent eruption, as was the case at Mt. Pelée. At St. Helens the great and destructive sideways blast followed development of a concealed dome. On the other hand, there is a dome activity forming at Santiaguito in Guatemala that started in 1922. As yet, no great eruption has resulted, and it is probable that the sticky lava just doesn't contain enough gases to produce explosive activity.

Each volcano has its own signature, and if volcanologists are to learn to predict eruptions, then they will have to learn to determine whether a given volcano system is competent to store sufficient energy to cause a large eruption. Then the same volcanologists will have to convince residents to leave the area—no easy task. Most people left the vicinity of St. Helens, but not all. At Mt. Pelée the authorities discounted the potential severity of the impending eruption because they wanted to hold an election and wanted the electrorate in town.

Although records are almost nonexistent, the eruption of Santorin, in the Aegean Sea, in about 1470 B.C., was seemingly anticipated by the residents of a town, Akrotiri, which has been slowly excavated by archaeologists over the past several decades. Apparently the area was shaken by two violent earthquakes which caused the residents to pack up and leave, for no bodies or easily portable belongings have been found at the site. Whether the people survived the eruption is not known, but it is clear that a giant eruption followed by a collapse into an emptied magma chamber caused the destruction of the Minoan civilization on Crete and is also thought to account for the legend of Atlantis, as many islands vanished into the sea forever. For

all we know, the people that fled Akrotiri might have
gotten to a place of safety and should be honored in the
history of volcanic events as one of the few groups who
really listened—when Vulcan spoke.

CHAPTER TEN

The View from Olympus

Field geology is a combination of close-up, detailed observations and broad, large-scale generalizations. Preparing a geologic map, a map that shows the areal distribution and mutual relations among rocks, is commonly the first step in unraveling the geologic history of a region. In order to be able to examine a large area for mapping, the field geologist depends a great deal on feet and a good pair of boots just to cover the ground. Any technique that reduces the time-consuming nature of mapping is eagerly sought and always has been.

In the days of the exploration of the lands west of the Mississippi there was an enormous area to be mapped and few people to do the mapping. The early geologists learned that the way to get an overall view of the geology in the West was to climb a prominent peak and have a look at it. In a land of canyons and ridges, a geologist in the bottom of a canyon saw only his immediate vicinity, but one on a mountaintop could see the great sweep of strata all around like a god looking down on pitiful Man from a mythical peak or land in the sky.

The geologist with a view could extrapolate things that

he had seen close up in the previous days and could see new features that warranted investigation. Many of the regions studied by the early geologists had not been mapped geographically, either, so a view from a peak gave a sense of spatial relations that could be obtained in no other way. The early USGS field men were excellent artists as well as first-rate scientists, for they had to record their observations as detailed sketches in field notebooks. The sketches are works of art by any standard as well as being almost photographically accurate. Indeed, modern-day researchers have used old sketches to evaluate changes in landforms and vegetation since the time of the original date.

One can imagine that even those pioneer field geologists on top of a peak or ridge looked longingly at the hawks and eagles that soared above their heads, literally getting a bird's eye view of the landscape, and pity the poor geologist trying to map in the plains, where there were no peaks to climb. Surely all of them wished for some godlike power to raise them from the ground so they could see their surroundings from on high. Hot-air balloons had been flown since 1783, and the Wright brothers had lifted off at Kill Devil Hills in 1903, but that wasn't of much use to the western geologists who worked from horseback out on the frontier.

The geologists' daydreams didn't become practical reality until World War I, when both the Germans and Allies used balloons and airplanes for reconnaissance flights over one another's territory. Even after World War I aerial observation didn't catch on with geologists in a big way. With the outbreak of World War II, the scene was set for large-scale aerial reconnaissance using photography. Much of the war was waged in places lacking adequate maps, and the military used photogrammetry to generate topographic maps of distant battlegrounds. By the end of the war, mapping by aerial photography was a standard procedure that brought most of the topographic surveyors out of the field and into darkened rooms where they stared at little glass-plate photos in stereovision.

Photogrammetry accelerated the production of topographic maps that geologists could use as bases for their geologic mapping, but it was the general availability of aerial photographs that was the biggest change. Aerial-photography programs were undertaken by the USGS, Forest Service, Bureau of Land Management, Department of Agriculture, and many other groups, including private companies. The photographs were primitive by today's standards, but they gave that aerial view that field geologists had been wanting for over a century of frustration. To be sure, the photos were in black and white and pretty fuzzy near the edges, but they allowed the field workers to see the trace of a geologic feature over many miles at a glance. The geologists could even pore over the photographs in their offices during the winter in preparation for forthcoming field seasons.

One added attraction of the photographs was that they were taken in lines of overlapping frames. Because of this fact, the mapper could use a stereoscopic viewer and see the ground in exaggerated relief with every valley and hill, every bump and wiggle, shown clearly. Geologists soon learned that they could use the photos with the unaided eye by looking walleyed at them, and stereovision of photographs became a required technique for geologists to learn.

Aerial photographs improved in quality as film and lenses became better, and airplanes became better guided and smoother flying. Improvements in resolution of lenses and film allowed for higher and higher flight paths, which reduced the need to correct for distortions, which were severe at low altitudes. Just as a close-up portrait of a person exaggerates the size of the nose, so are the shapes of peaks and valleys distorted in a low-altitude aerial photograph. Less distorted photographs from high altitudes result from the greater camera-to-subject distance, not from

better lenses, just as a skilled photographer will use a
telephoto lens for portraits to eliminate the bulgy nose
problem. The better lenses merely allow better resolution,
not necessarily lower distortion. As a natural consequence
of its great utility in many fields, aerial photography became relatively inexpensive and of high quality.

The urge to get up high that the old-timers had when
they looked at the birds wasn't quenched by improvements
in planes and photographic techniques. People still wanted
better photographs. The desire was particularly strong with
the military, which wanted to know what was going on
inside the Soviet Union, China, Korea, and other parts of
the world that were inaccessible during the Cold War of
the 1950s.

Supercameras were mounted in the secret U-2 plane
that could fly very high. The military wouldn't say how
high, but it was assumed that heights of about 30,000
meters (100,000 feet) were usual. After the Soviets shot
down a U-2 over its territory and captured the pilot, there
was no use keeping much in the way of secrets. It became
common knowledge that the quality of photographs from
a U-2 platform was such that the white lines in a parking
lot could be resolved.

Still the hunger for better detail from on high was not
satisfied. Cameras were sent into space to get an even more
sweeping look at the earth's surface. The first images that
became available to the civilian world weren't very exciting.
The area covered was wonderful, but the resolution was
dismal. Every piece of information had to be sent to earth
by radio telemetry, and the images were patchwork quilts
of shades of gray. With improvements, the quilts began to
look more and more like photographs.

In addition to improved resolution, which meant more
detail, the cameras in space gathered their information in
several different wavelengths, including some outside the
visible part of the spectrum. Color photographs could be

synthesized from the satellite images, including so-called false images on which the infrared part of the spectrum is reproduced as red. Infrared radiation is reflected very effectively by plants, and the false color images were used by foresters, agricultural researchers, and botanists as well as geologists.

The first major use of satellite-borne imaging for the nonmilitary market was by the National Aeronautics and Space Administration (NASA) in the Earth Resources Technology Satellite (ERTS) program. Research at university and government laboratories flourished with the wide availability of ERTS imagery and NASA funding.

ERTS, later called Landsat, images had one tremendous advantage over conventional aerial photography, even from a U-2, which was that they were distortion-free. That was readily accomplished because the data that were used to make up the images were already in numerical form that could be processed by computers to remove distortion or present the data in any map projection that was needed. From a little stack of Landsat images a map maker could produce an accurate map of a city or state without ever leaving the office.

Given digital data and a computer, researchers couldn't leave well enough alone, and they developed techniques to make the images better by messing with the data—so-called enhancement. Enhancement is a sophisticated art that I'll leave to the specialists, but one wonders how an imagine can be made better than the original—a feat that sounds impossible on the face of it. The basic information is the intensity of light of a given range of wavelengths over a given area of the image. One form of enhancement is to fill in missing data or correct wrong data. If a given piece of the picture quilt, called a pixel, is missing, then the quality of the picture is reduced. If a lot of pixels are missing, the picture may resemble "snowy" reception of a TV set. Such missing data can be reconstructed by a computer, which compares the data for a given blank pixel of the picture with the data for all surrounding pixels. In the simplest case, the missing data are filled in with an average value of the surrounding pieces, and the "snow" disappears. To further increase resolution of an image, the number of pixels can be increased by the computer. That is comparable in a way to using a finer-grained photographic film to get a sharper picture. The computer does the job by generating extra pixels at the intersection of the original ones. Thus, the graininess of the image is cut in half. The false data for the new pixels are just the average of the four pixels that intersect at a point in the quilt.

Another trick is to increase the contrast of an image with a computer. Satellite images have a huge range in intensity because the images must be adequate in brightly lit parts of the terrain surveyed as well as in darkened portions such as canyons or the shadowy side of hills. The result of this wide range is images that lack contrast. The photographic enhancer must study the range of wavelengths of interest in the data to determine which spectral bands contain most of the picture information. Then that range is "stretched" by the computer to fill the normal range of the photographic image which is the output. A skilled photographer does a similar thing in the darkroom by exposing different parts of the photographic paper for different times to draw useful images out of dark and bright portions of the print, a process done by automatic equipment in some photo labs.

Other skulduggery performed by the computer includes presentation of data as ratios between spectral bands rather than the raw data, which can have remarkably positive effects on the images. Another trick is to have the computer emphasize small-scale differences in the image over large-scale differences by so-called electronic filtering. That has the effect of emphasizing fine detail, with an overall improvement in apparent image sharpness.

Lest we get lost in the world of data processing and

forget the old-fashioned camera, it is still a fact that ordinary photographs are higher-quality images than those produced from digital data, no matter how much enhancement has been visited upon it. The limit is set by the size of the areas on the ground represented by one pixel. For Landsat imagery the area is about 60 by 80 meters (200 by 250 feet), a size that means that an average dwelling would not be resolved, though a stadium or shopping mall might be. The photographs taken by cameras in Skylab and other vehicles have been widely published, and their excellent quality is obvious to anyone. The geologist wanting to use images for mapping would generally still rely on aerial photographs taken from airplanes because of their higher resolution.

I did some combined laboratory and field studies of imagery of the Wind River Mountains in Wyoming. I used natural-color aircraft images from conventional aircraft, black-and-white U-2 photographs, Skylab photographs, and Landsat images. High technology nothwithstanding, the color aerial photographs were by far the most useful for general mapping, discrimination between rock types, and delineation of features of the region. The Landsat images and Skylab photographs were valuable for regional patterns but of limited use for detail. The combination of regional images and conventional aerial photography provided a rich tray of information. At the present state of the art, however, aerial photographs are still the most useful sort of image to a geologist.

Such a comparison is missing part of the point of imagery, however, because photographs are limited to images in the visible portion of the light spectrum plus a bit of the infrared. If the gods on Olympus were really gods, then they must have been able to see more information than ordinary mortals. So also can we look at the earth and other objects in space in ways other than the plainly visible.

The electromagnetic spectrum ranges from long-

wavelength radio waves to the most energetic X rays. Our
ability to utilize radiation depends mainly on two factors:
the ability of the radiation to penetrate the atmosphere
and the technical feasibility of detecting the radiation.
Energetic X rays penetrate the atmosphere readily, but
there is not enough incident X-ray energy striking the earth
to "illuminate" it—a fact that we can be thankful for.
Lower-energy X rays and ultraviolet light are plentifully
supplied from the sun but are absorbed in the atmosphere. Apart from visible light, the only parts of the spectrum that can penerate the atmosphere are parts of the
infrared and the longer wavelength thermal infrared (such
as one feels from a hot stove). There is strong absorption
of many portions of the infrared spectrum, including all
of the very long infrared that bridges the gap to radio
waves. With microwaves, the wavelength used for radar,
and all the rest of the radio spectrum, absorption is minimal. Thus, portions of the infrared and the radio spectra
are useful.

Detection of infrared has become highly sophisticated
in the past decades, as has detection of microwave radiation. Detectors of either type of radiation can also be
physically small, a fact of great importance to both scientists and police officers catching speed demons in radar
traps. For wavelengths longer than microwaves the size
of detectors that are necessary to achieve useful resolution
is far too great to allow their mounting on a satellite or
aircraft.

Infrared and microwaves have one essential difference
besides difference in wavelengths. For infrared images
there is plenty of natural radiation that illuminates the
earth. With microwaves the energy must be provided in
the form of a radar transmitter producing radiation that
reflects from the surface.

Radar images have proved useful in a number of applications. For one thing, clouds are transparent to micro-

waves for the most part, so radar images are useful where almost continuous cloud cover is found, as in many mountainous regions. Because of their long wavelength, microwaves theoretically can't give as high a resolution as infrared or visible light, but the practical resolution is controlled by other factors such as pixel size, so that the difference is not as great as one might imagine from the difference in wavelengths. (Microwaves have a wavelength more than a thousand times that of infrared.) Microwaves are able to provide more information than visible light under some conditions. The scattering of microwaves is strongly dependent on the texture of the reflecting surface, with the result that objects on the ground that could look the same under visible light look very different by radar. For example, a rough, blocky lava flow might appear identical to a smooth one in a light image, but a radar image would distinguish them. In the same way, radar would allow distinction of sand from gravel because of differences in the smoothness of the surface underlain by each.

Microwave radiation even has the ability to penetrate dry sand, and radar images of some desert areas of Egypt have displayed long-abandoned river-drainage patterns that are not visible in other ways. Buried features have also been discovered in the Mojave Desert of California. The penetrating ability of microwaves offers great promise for geological surveying in sand-covered terrain as well as discovery and mapping of buried archaeological sites in such regions.

Infrared sensing has been used to produce images much like those from visible light but until recently has had relatively minor application in geologic work except as a guide to vegetation character. It had long been known that many minerals have distinctive absorption spectra for infrared radiation and that infrared spectroscopy can be used to characterize rock samples in the laboratory. Recently, Alexander Goetz of the Jet Propulsion Laboratory and his co-workers have devised an infrared spectrometer that can be used for imaging from satellites or aircraft. The common minerals of the earth's crust, feldspar and quartz, have no distinctive reflectance spectra, but other minerals, especially clays and carbonate minerals, have characteristic patterns. In a test aerial survey over the Cuprite mining district in Nevada, the spectrometer was able to distinguish two contrasting areas of altered rock in a mineralized region from the reflection spectra of two minerals. Altered rocks are frequently associated with ore deposits, so the potential of mapping their distribution by remote sensing is most exciting to economic geologists.

Present trends in remote sensing in geology are to use aircraft images rather than satellite ones. There are a couple of reasons for this. The obvious one is resolution. With an imaging system that produces 60-by-80-meter pixels from space, one can use an aircraft as a platform and get both high resolution and the benefit of digital data that can be processed in various ways by computers to squeeze out more information. In addition, the aircraft-mounted devices can provide information for a huge range of wavelengths not accessible to cameras and film.

The other reason for using aircraft is secrecy. I don't mean military secrecy but industrial secrecy. With satellite data, everyone has equal access, provided they can come up with the modest charges to buy the imagery. With aircraft-mounted sensors an exploration company can survey a region and keep the information private for the exclusive use of their staff. Such competitive work has lead to less expensive equipment in the past as instrumentation companies vie for their piece of the market. One can hope that competition in sensing of the earth will provide new and different data to exploration geologist and academic alike.

Lest you get the idea that remote sensing of the earth

has become a highly developed science since the days of the lonely USGS geologist making a sketch from the top of a peak, let me assure you that there is still a lot of pretty basic sensing going on. Geologists still do a lot of riding in four-wheel-drive vehicles and wear out a lot of boots. As recently as the 1970s one private company employed a geologist to collect plant samples for a geochemical survey while he dangled at treetop height from a rope held aloft by a helicopter. A USGS geologist-pilot surveyed an area in Alaska from a light plane, collecting samples by throwing various gadgets out of the plane on ropes which were later pulled in by hand. One of his devices was a ball covered with putty that would adhere to rock fragments on the ground so they could be reeled in. This "sticky ball," the official name, obviously owes its heritage to the age-old practice of kids trying to recover change from beneath street gratings with a wad of bubble gum on a string.

So it is that science and technology march on with multi-million-dollar instruments competing with sticky balls to relieve the geologist of a blister or two. It is most fortunate that any survey from the air or from space is still only preliminary and that a geologist still has to tread the ground to get the whole story. If geology ever abandons field work, the science will be on the way out, because it is just the out-of-doors nature of the work that makes geology an appealing discipline to a large portion of its practitioners. Many of the greats in the history of geology have been people who turned to geology instead of chemistry or physics not only because they liked physical science but because they also liked to be in the mountains and deserts and along the coastlines and rivers of the world, grappling with the truly great and vast problems of earth in their native and natural habitat instead of in a mind-confining building. Moreover, lunch from a brown bag eaten under an ancient tree on a ridge top by a rushing

creek is a whole lot better than leaving a darkened office
to eat in a cafeteria or faculty lounge even if one's lunch
companion by the tree may just be a jay or a chipmunk. At
least they don't run football pools or try to collect money
for retiring cohorts.

CHAPTER ELEVEN

Salt Rising

Massive bodies of rock salt are found throughout the world in a great variety of geologic settings. Most such bodies are made of sodium chloride (halite or common table salt), though many also contain sylvite (potassium chloride) as an important constituent. These minerals are associated with magnesium chlorides, sulfates, and various minor minerals in deposits known collectively as evaporites because they formed from the evaporation of water, generally seawater. As I mentioned in the essay "Boron 93516," there are also numerous evaporites that result from evaporation of saline lake waters, but we'll consider marine evaporites here, and particularly those composed largely of halite.

Most rock-salt deposits are in the form of thick layers within sequences of ordinary sedimentary rocks. In such geologic settings, mines have been opened to exploit vast reserves of salt for the table and almost endless industrial uses. Salt mines get bad press, with phrases such as "back to the salt mines" used to epitomize a return to difficult drudgery. Supposedly, the ultimate punishment in the Soviet Union is to be sent to the salt mines of Siberia. I have never been to Siberia, but I have been in salt mines and can report that they without doubt offer vastly more pleasant working conditions than any other sort of mine that I'm familiar with. They are dry, clean, and well lighted and are free of the usual dangers of mining, such as collapse of the ceiling rocks, poisonous gases, and explosions.

Geologist Raphael Pumpelly tells in his *Reminiscences* of visiting a salt mine in 1858 near Wielicksin in what was then Austrian Poland, where, one thousand feet below the surface "There was an enormous salon with a table cut out of the rock (salt) running the whole length of the rooms. Chandeliers hung from the roof, with pendants of salt crystals instead of glass, and the walls were, I think, decorated with sculptures in the same glistening material. In this room, I was told, there had been a royal banquet." I can imagine that mining salt by hand is hard work, but in today's mines all the labor is done by huge machines guided by miners working in all the discomfort of a German businessman driving his Mercedes down the Autobahn.

Salt mines offer such stable and clean environments that abandoned ones are routinely used for storage of valuable records, foodstuffs, manufactured items, and other things needing a safe repository. Man-made openings in salt deposits have even been suggested as secure repositories for radioactive wastes of various sorts and are in use for that purpose by Sweden.

Most salt mines are underground, but in some parts of the world there are surface exposures of rock salt. As you might surmise, salt deposits at the surface are mostly confined to places with dry climates, although that is not really an essential element for their persistence, as we will see. Some salt bodies are even exposed on the floor of saline bodies of water. The saturated solution surrounding these bodies cannot dissolve any more salt than it already holds, so they persist.

Most of the surface deposits of salt are exposures of so-called salt domes, columnar or mushroom-shaped masses of rock salt that have moved upward from their source in a salt layer, penetrating and shoving aside the overlying rocks. With some salt domes, not only does the column of salt rise all the way to the surface, but a few even have glacierlike salt bodies downhill from the main salt mass.

The first salt dome was recognized, insofar as the published literature is a guide, in 1856, at a place called Rang el Melah (salt mountain) in Algeria, where a French mining engineer, E. Ville, observed that the salt actually penetrated through the sedimentary rocks that surrounded it rather than just forming a layer within them. Ville and various geologists soon found many more salt-cored structures along the Atlas Mountains and mentioned the "eruptive and geyser-like behavior" of the salt, forming what geologists today call diapiric structures. Salt domes are common in both Europe and North America, but even where they reach the surface, their true nature is concealed by water or by accumulated insoluble residue left behind by centuries of solution of the salt. Even though salt has been mined in Europe for centuries, the character of the columnar domes had seemingly not been ascertained until Engineer Ville visited Algeria.

As with any new discovery, a proliferation of discoveries of salt domes in other parts of the world followed, along with an equal proliferation of hypotheses to account for their formation. Everyone recognized from the geologic relationships of the salt and the surrounding rocks that the rock salt had behaved plastically as it emplaced itself into overlying rocks, but details of the mechanism were not agreed upon. An early view was that the weight of the overlying rocks somehow squeezed the mobile salt upward. Then, in 1912, the Swedish scientist Arrhenius proposed that salt bodies rose buoyantly into overlying strata because their density was less than the other rocks. The great structural geologist from Hanover and later Göttingen, Stille, maintained that the salt was caused to rise by the same tangential forces acting in the earth's crust that he thought caused mountain building and other related pro-

cesses. Other geologists thought that pressure from crystallization, with an increase in volume, caused the salt to move
to regions of lower pressure in an upward direction. A controversy about salt diapirs raged in Europe during the first
few decades of this century but went largely unnoticed in
the United States because the arguments were published in
German and American scientists were as inept at foreign
languages then as now.

In 1917 a USGS geologist named Eugene Wesley Shaw
proposed that salt diapirs in the Gulf Coast somehow rose
by differential pressure arising from the weight of overlying
sediments. Shaw had proposed in 1913 that diapiric bodies
of soft mud, so-called mud lumps, found in the delta of the
Mississippi, formed by the same mechanism. Shaw further
proposed that salt domes could be found by measuring the
strength of gravity over them and the surrounding rocks
because the density of rock salt was greater than that of
the soft, unconsolidated sediments near the surface around
salt domes. Shaw apparently misunderstood that rock salt
is considerably less dense than ordinary sedimentary rocks,
not more dense. As it happened, his idea went untested
because in those days gravity measurements in the field were
made by counting the rate of swinging of a pendulum, a
cumbersome method, to say the least. Modern gravimeters
are simpler and much more sensitive than those of Shaw's
time and are used to locate salt domes. The salt domes
underlie regions of lesser—not greater—pull of gravity.

Information about the structure of salt domes and the
surrounding rocks accumulated through the years for two
reasons. For one, many domes were mined for their salt,
and the mining allowed geologists a detailed look at the
internal structures of the salt dome. In addition, there are
petroleum accumulations associated with many salt domes
in the domed sediments over the salt as well as in upturned
layers that are truncated by the salt mass. For that reason
there was a wealth of detail gathered about the structure
of the enclosing sediments from numerous drill-hole records.

Here, then, was a geologic phenomenon with almost un-paralleled data available from many sources. The laboratory called Earth had provided geologists with many experiments that provided evidence that salt masses had moved upward, penetrating overlying rocks. An explanation of the whole salt-diapir mechanism was close at hand, but the details were still a matter for serious disagreement among specialists.

One detail not settled was how rock salt was able to be-have plastically, almost like a very viscous liquid. If halite is struck with a hammer, it breaks into many tiny cleavage fragments with right-angle edges and corners. If a block of rock salt is squeezed slowly, it also eventually fails by brittle fracture rather than by flow. By contrast, sylvite, the potas-sium analogue of halite, is a ductile material under ordinary surface conditions. If a knife blade is drawn across a piece of sylvite, it cuts a smooth grove, with the removed material formed into ridges on either side, as would happen with a soft, ductile metal. Since halite isn't ductile in that sense, a knife-scratch test is used as one means of distinguishing the two in a hand specimen.

With metals, the classic ductile substances, the degree of brittleness or ductility is strongly dependent on tempera-ture, with ductile behavior favored by high temperature and brittleness by low ones. The same relationship holds for other crystalline materials such as rocks, and also for rock salt. Experiments showed that halite was very ductile at 150°C and behaved like a viscous fluid at 300 degrees. Obviously, high temperatures in the source region of a salt dome would favor the plastic flow indicated by the internal and external features of natural examples.

The internal structure of halite, the first crystal structure ever determined by the use of the diffraction of X rays in the first years of this century, is made up of chlorine and sodium ions (an ion is a charged atom) arranged as if they were located at the corners of a cube, with every other corner occupied by sodium, then chlorine, and so forth. Another way to visualize the structure is to picture layers of alternating sodiums and chlorines arranged in a square pattern like a chessboard. Those layers are stacked one atop the other, with chlorines over sodiums and vice versa, in the same way as a three-dimensional chess game. The result is a cubic array of alternating sodium and chlorine atoms. Experimental studies showed that halite deformed plastically by sliding of the layers of sodium and chloride atoms over one another in directions parallel to the cube-face directions in the crystal. That means there are three planes at right angles to one another in a halite crystal along which the crystal can deform by the layers slipping or sliding across one another without the crystal breaking. Thus, for any given crystal subjected to external force, it is likely that one of the three directions will be oriented suitably with respect to the external force so that sliding can occur.

The sliding, or gliding as it is also called, parallel to a cube-face direction also provides a reason why sylvite deforms in a ductile or plastic way more readily than halite. Chlorine ions are about 50 percent larger than sodium ions but are about the same size as potassium ions. The layers of ions parallel to the cube faces are arranged so that both columns and rows of ions alternate chlorines and either sodium in halite or potassium in sylvite. Inasmuch as the chlorine and potassium are roughly the same size the cube-face planes are less "bumpy" than in the case of a cube-face plane in halite, so the sylvite planes can slide across one another more readily. All of these properties of halite and sylvite apply to the pure materials under dry conditions, an unlikely natural condition in a world where water is almost ubiquitous.

It had been known to geologists and others since almost the beginning of the present century that rock salt deformed in a much more ductile way when it was immersed in water or even just wet, a phenomenon known as the Joffée effect. The explanation of the effect was that the surface layers of halite absorb gases from the atmosphere and the presence of the extra atoms inhibits the gliding of one layer over another, the surface thereby becoming hardened. The hardened outer layers then inhibit overall ductile deformation of the salt. The presence of water frees the contaminants from the surface layers of the halite so it can deform more plastically.

With this information at hand, L. L. Nettleton, a geophysicist with Gulf Research and Development, used scale models to make miniature, salt-dome-like structures in the laboratory. He used viscous fluids instead of rock salt and sedimentary rocks and produced close imitations of salt domes with no external forces other than the differential pull of gravity on substances of different density. Nettleton's analysis was really a return to the original ideas of Arrhenius, with experiments and some modern data added. Emplacement of most salt domes by buoyant rising of the salt became generally accepted after Nettleton's work was published in 1934.

There was still no explanation for the salt often found in the core of anticlines, convex-upward wrinkles in the layered rocks of the earth. The sticky point was that Stille's followers thought that folding into anticlines caused the salt to move and thicken in the cores of the folds. They argued that there was no mechanism for a smooth layer of salt to start to flow upward at some point unless the rocks had been squeezed and bent by external forces. It was a chicken/egg argument. Did the anticlines make the salt domes, or did the rising of salt localize formation of anticlines?

In 1960, geologist F. Trusheim, exploration manager for a German oil company, published a paper showing that salt domes could form directly from a salt layer, but only after the layer had developed thickened parts he called pillows. Once pillows had formed, then the salt began its rise. As to the ease with which salt could move, Trusheim noted that the salt in German potash mines moved as much as a meter a year to close up openings left by mining.

Given that and more information, geologist W. C. Gus-

sow, then with the Union Oil research center, wrote a remarkably dogmatic paper in 1966 in which he stated that
the motivating force for all intrusions, salt or otherwise, is
the weight of the overlying rocks; that salt domes are never
found in places where the source evaporite layers are shallower than 15,000 feet (4,600 meters); and that it is physically impossible for salt to flow at the surface under
atmospheric temperature and pressure. Therefore, he concluded, salt glaciers must have been extruded onto the
surface in a hot condition. Gussow's return to early-
twentieth-century ideas was a puzzling position to be taken
just twenty years ago, but it does illustrate how slowly old
and discredited ideas go away.

Experimental evidence has shown that environmental
pressure has little or no effect on the behavior of rock salt,
so burial cannot be deemed vital insofar as it provides a
high-pressure environment. Burial does of course mean
that the rock salt will be in a higher temperature regime,
because temperatures in the crust increase downward at a
rate in the range of 8 to 40°C per kilometer of depth. Therefore, burial could increase ductility by the temperature
effect.

Alas, the statement that the source layer of salt domes
must be deeper than 15,000 feet doesn't stand up to the
geologic evidence. There is evidence from the North Sea
and the Mississippi Valley that salt movement started when
only a few hundred meters of sediment buried the evaporites. This can be determined because the domes were already bulging the sea floor as sediments were being deposited,
so the sediments are thinner over the dome than away from
it. In Arizona there appears to be modern upward movement of salt under a cover of only 150 to 300 meters (500
to 1,000 feet). More damaging yet to Gussow's dogma is a
salt pan, a shallow basin filled with evaporites, in Ethiopia,
where domes of halite breach the surface under a condition
of zero cover.

A leading student of salt domes, Christopher J. Talbot of the University of Dundee, now at Uppsala, Sweden, examined the effects of temperature on salt behavior and concluded that the Ethiopian shallow salt domes are the result of unusually high local heat flow in the region, resulting in increased ductility and plastic flow within the salt. He proposes that under temperatures up to a couple of hundred degrees the salt bodies would undergo convection, the process whereby warm material rises and cold material sinks. According to Talbot, the convection process in a rock-salt layer would take place in domains with a hot center portion rising and cooled material sinking down the sides. Talbot also points out that rock salt is about ten times as heat conductive as ordinary sedimentary rocks. Thus, a sedimentary cover would have a heat-blanketing effect and serve to help the temperature in a buried salt body increase. Once salt bodies began to ascend to the surface after starting out as convecting bodies, their low density would add its buoyant effect to help their rise. At some point, emplaced salt bodies would act as thermal conduits to drain off excess heat and stop active convection, a stage that could be reached whether or not the salt breached the surface. Talbot suggests that thermal convection of salt would take place only in regions of abnormally high heat flow from the interior and that an equilibrium would be reached when enough heat was drained to the surface through the salt-dome conductors.

Salt layers are rare in Precambrian rocks (older than 590 million years), and what is found is in rocks that are late Precambrian and which appear to have undergone little metamorphism. There is also a rough increase in rock-salt layers with decreasing age of the enclosing sediments, although there are times in earth history when salt deposition was more important than in others. Gussow argued that the age distribution of salt indicated that it had been melted and forced out of old rocks. A less dramatic view

might be that given enough time, salt tends to rise through
the crust and leave its source layer, perhaps aided by heating, but not to the extent that a salt lava is formed.

As to the physical impossibility of salt glaciers flowing
under surface conditions of temperature and pressure, we
can look to Talbot again. Gussow based his assertion on
the laboratory behavior of salt under most unnatural conditions. The earth is a much more reliable laboratory for
the bulk of geologic questions, and Talbot and a colleague,
Eric Rogers, studied salt glaciers emerging from an exposed
salt dome at Kuh-e-Namak, Dashti, in southwest Iran. Kuh-
e-Namak means salt mountain in Farsi, and there are so
many salt mountains in the Zagros mountain belt that the
province name is usually tagged on at the end to distinguish
which Kuh-e-Namak is meant.

At "their" salt mountain, Talbot and Rogers painted
stripes across an apparently active salt glacier and also surveyed in a number of points to observe any movement.
They returned to study the glacier several times after intervals of months and found that the glacier was indeed
actively moving under ordinary conditions. The formerly
straight stripes were curved and wrinkled, and their survey
points had undergone substantial migration. They also
observed that the salt glacier would begin to move when
as little as a few millimeters of rain fell on it and that after
a rainfall movement continued for a couple of days. Gussow's idea that the salt was erupted hot and that the glaciers
were remnants of salt-lava flows was not correct. Talbot
planned more work at the site, but the deteriorating Iranian
political climate in 1978 convinced him to terminate his
work in the field.

Happily, enough information had been gathered during
his field work to give him plenty of grist for the mill of
science. Talbot put together a theoretical model for the
dynamics of the salt dome and its associated salt glaciers.
By making a number of reasonable assumptions based on
established physical laws and his field observations, Talbot

was able to calculate a budget for the actively moving salt body. He found that it was most reasonable to assume that the active salt glacier was being replenished at the top by new salt from the rising dome as salt was removed at the bottom of the glacier and along its upper surface by solution and avalanching. It was no surprise that the model showed that the dome was active and that the glacier was moving, because his field evidence supported that view. One consequence of the model was surprising indeed. At Kuh-e-Namak the annual rainfall is about 28 centimeters (11 inches)— pretty dry. The surprise was that it appeared that the salt dome would be exposed at the surface even if the rainfall was as much as 67 centimeters/year (26 inches/year). That meant that an active salt dome could survive at the surface almost anywhere except regions of unusually high rainfall. Gussow notwithstanding, there are active salt glaciers in Iran and could be in other regions under similar circumstances.

One additional item of interest about the salt diapirs of the Zagros Mountains is that there is a line of them with the old, apparently inactive ones at the north, with successively younger ones to the south. The one Talbot studied is seemingly the most active of the line of domes. Twenty kilometers (12 miles) south of Kuh-e-Namak is Kuh-e-Darang, a fold mountain with a salt core that has not yet emerged and may not have even pierced the overlying sediments yet. Talbot doesn't suggest it, but one wonders if the southward migration of salt activity with time might be attributed to the sliding of the whole mass of enclosing sediments northward over a region of abnormally high heat flow, much in the same way the crust under the Hawaiian chain is thought to have moved across a hot spot in the underlying mantle. In Iran and surrounding regions there are numerous localities with higher-than-normal heat flow, so a buried one under Kuh-e-Darang is not unreasonable. Convection would begin in the salt over the hot place, which would initiate the upward flow of the salt. Continued rising would proceed by buoyant rise. It is also reasonable that the sheet of sediments is crumpling to the north as the Arabian plate pushes against the Eurasian plate in that structurally active part of the earth. Talbot attributes the line to a deep structure that gave rise to pillows of salt that initiated the dome. He also states that it is reasonable to assume that pressure from the folding activity in the area plays a role in dome formation as well as buoyant rising of the mass.

Talbot's study is a classic by any standard, and one can hope that he is able to continue his Iranian work at some time when being an Englishman is a bit more politically acceptable in Iran than at present. Salt-dome studies in general are of a great deal of interest to geologists, for they serve as models for emplacement of other rock bodies, including masses of granite and the layered granites called granite gneisses.

In many highly metamorphosed terranes (groups of related rocks), domelike bodies of granite gneiss appear to penetrate surrounding metamorphic rocks to form what are termed mantled gneiss domes. Many geologists think that mantled gneiss domes are diapiric bodies of layered gneiss that have risen buoyantly through overlying metamorphic rocks now found draped over the gneisses in much the same way that sediments drape over salt domes. Gneiss has a lower density than average crustal rock, so it would be able to rise buoyantly, just as a mass of salt can do.

Looking at a gneiss dome in the field, one can certainly see the reasoning that supports such an idea, but gneiss is a far cry from a ductile rock under any surface conditions. However, the gneiss domes probably were emplaced when the gneiss was at a temperature in the range of 400 to 600°C. At that temperature, a gneiss would be partly melted and would certainly behave plastically. Perhaps even a lower temperature would be sufficient to allow the gneiss to move.

In addition, many geologists think that granite gneisses

develop from other rocks by addition of alkalies (sodium, potassium) and silica. A fraction of all natural potassium is composed of the radioactive isotope ^{40}K, so a gneiss would contain a built-in heat source from the radioactive potassium. Rocks of granitic composition, such as granite gneisses, are also especially rich in radioactive uranium and thorium. Moreover, gneiss domes are found in rocks of great antiquity, mostly in the billion-year-old and older range. Consider that their antiquity means that when the domes were forming, the rocks contained a considerably greater amount of radioactive elements than at present because a significant fraction of those elements had not decayed yet. Local heat from radioactivity may have been instrumental in raising the temperature of the gneissic rocks to permit their emplacement as diapiric masses.

Ordinary granites may well be emplaced in the same manner as salt domes and gneiss domes. With granites that form from the cooling and crystallization of a molten mass, there is no problem about mobility. Molten granite would be a very viscous liquid, but easily capable of rising through the crust buoyantly. Field evidence in many places indicates that granites are emplaced by shoving aside and penetrating overlying rocks, just as with salt domes. In addition, because it is a liquid, chunks of the invaded, higher-density rock can fall into the melt and sink to allow space for the granite to rise.

Granites, like salt domes, also penetrate to the surface in many regions, but instead of salt glaciers, they give rise to outpourings of lava and other volcanic rocks, and often to volcanoes. Unlike rock salt, granite melts are filled with water and other gases, so the surface expulsion of rock may be considerably more violent, but the basic mechanisms are broadly similar. No doubt many bodies of granite and rock salt are emplaced under a driving pressure from crustal movement or from the weight of overlying rock, but it is probable that the most important driving force is just plain gravity, with the less dense floating through the more dense.

In the broadest sense, the original continental crust evolved through upward emplacement of low-density granitic rocks and downward displacement of higher-density rocks more like basalts.

The primitive continental crust was probably formed by a process not much more complicated than the formation of the crust in a cake my mother used to make. She would line a cake pan with a dough, then pour a mixture of berries over the top. The whole thing went into the oven that way, then emerged after baking with the crust on the top and the berries on the bottom. The dough had little streaks of purple in it to show where it had dragged against the berry mix on its upward trip. It was a fine example of one material of low density rising through another of higher density. Not only that—it was delicious.

CHAPTER TWELVE

The .07 Percent Solution

It has always been interesting to me how language reflects the geography of the region where it arose. Icelandic is rich in words describing landforms, with terms for different sorts of hills, slopes, valleys, and the like reflecting the rich variation in that lightly vegetated land. Norwegian has many terms for islands, submerged rocks, inlets, and other matters relating to Norway's deeply incised and complex shoreline. Mountaineering terms originate mostly from the French and flatland words from Russian. It comes as no surprise that Serbo-Croatian has an almost baroque vocabulary of words relating to limestone caves.

Perhaps I'm being unfair to say that anything in Serbo-Croatian comes as no surprise to anyone but a Serb or a Croat, but it is a fact that the most famous region of caves and sinkholes in the world is in Yugoslavia (and adjacent Italy), with suitable words to go with the features. The word karst, used to describe the typical terrain, is derived from the Slavic word *kras*, or *krs*, and the Italian word *carso*, the Italian word meaning "bleak, waterless place."

Prof. J. Cvijić wrote a classic paper on karst in 1893 using the terms doline, poljes, uvalas, and ponor for slightly dif-

151

ferent sorts of depressions in the surface. But even the Slavic Cvijić chides the Serbo-Croatians for using *vrtaca, ponikva, vrtlina, do, dolac, duliba,* and *dolina* to describe trivial variations of the English sinkhole. Furthermore, if the holes lead to caves, they are *besdno, stromor, zwekara, jama,* and *luknja.* French is at least as rich, or perhaps cluttered is a better word, with words to describe the karst terrains west of the Rhone River. Cvijić even borrowed a French term *lapiez* for terrains cut by numerous narrow, deep fissures parallel to one another over which travel is difficult or impossible. I will stick with my native English, even though sinkhole is essentially the only name for almost all of the words above.

Karst regions are underlain by water-soluble rock, principally limestone and dolomite. Limestone is composed mostly of the mineral calcite, which is calcium carbonate. Dolomite the rock is composed of dolomite the mineral, calcium magnesium carbonate, with some calcite. In many places the rock is bare and soil-free, with characteristic deep cracks, pits, and irregularities. Caves, or at the very least a complex system of fissures, underlie most karst regions. As a consequence, surface drainage of water is the exception, not the rule. What surface flow is present is uniquely karst-like. Streams flow down valleys only to vanish into holes in the ground. Streams also commonly appear from such holes and flow down stream-cut valleys, forming what the old western movies called box canyons. Some karst upwellings are very large indeed and are as a class the largest springs in the world.

The public knowledge of karst is generally restricted to news items about sinkholes collapsing and swallowing houses in Florida and to visits to, or pictures of, commercially developed caves. Caves are also thought of as places where towering stalactites and stalagmites and masses of sparkling crystals adorn the ceilings, floors, and walls. In years past, caves were also places where people got lost, and national attention would be riveted on search parties wandering without success in a labyrinth of passageways.

For some reason, people don't get lost in caves anymore. Perhaps it is because *Tom Sawyer* isn't very popular reading these days. Maybe it is because so many caves are commercialized or operated as public parks. My guess is that people have simply lost interest in exploring caves except for that small group of devotees called spelunkers and their scientific offshoot the speleologists. Because of the organized spelunkers even the minor caves are mapped in detail, so ordinary people simply have a hard time getting lost or can be found quickly if they do take a wrong turn in the dark. Recently in Texas three kids who had just seen Steven Spielberg's film *Goonies* were inspired by the celluloid teenaged cave explorers to visit a local cave. One of the kids got trapped and was promptly rescued by a group called Texas Cave Rescue, which then filled in the cave entrance. And adults complain that kids never do anything but sit in front of the boob tube.

The focus on stalactites, stalagmites, and all the other "ites" in caves gives a very false view of caves. Such features are produced by the deposition of calcite in the caves. Yet caves are products of solution of the rock, not deposition of new rock. It's like visiting the New York subway and marveling at the graffiti or the Moscow subway and admiring the tile work when the real wonder is the engineering and construction of the great tubes beneath the surface. It is the formation of the caves, not their decoration, that should be of interest. Geologists are no better than the general public in this regard. I may have missed a book, but I know of no beginning geology textbook that shows a picture of a plain cave without the window dressing; they invariably show a photo taken in Carlsbad, Mammoth, Luray, or some other cavern with showy stalactites and stalagmites. Human nature is what it is, however, and I recall visiting Wind Cave in the Black Hills and listening to the grumbling of

tourists who expected the traditional cave "formations" and
saw only bare, plain rock. They wanted a pretty cave, not
just any cave: "What's the government doing running a
cave like this with taxpayers' money?" I recall one saying.

And sinkholes, apart from their news value when a house
vanishes into one, are usually nuisances to farmers in Indiana, Illinois, and other places where they dot the landscape. Farm animals fall down them, so they have to be
fenced, but sinkholes do make handy places to dump garbage or manure. Never mind that the dumped garbage
goes directly into the groundwater being pumped up for
domestic use in the vicinity.

Caves have been home to ancient man and many animals
before and after man's appearance on the scene. Priceless
fossils have been found in old cave deposits. Valuable
petroleum reserves have filled underground caverns near
Vera Cruz, Mexico. Many a fine cheese or wine owes its per-
fection to storage in the constant conditions of a natural
cave. I say that caves are fine things. Also, their mode of
formation offers some neatly packaged lessons in geology
and geochemistry, lessons that are mostly presented incorrectly in leading textbooks. So cast aside preconceived no-
tions and we will examine the genesis of karst.

Cvijić's paper on karst, "Das Karstphanomen," published
in 1893, gave karst studies real scientific status. Previously,
most geologists and geographers had regarded karst as just
an interesting, if trivial, curiosity. Cvijić's central theme was
that karst formed from surface effects on soluble rocks and
that the variety of features owed their origin to solution
from the top downward.

As with most scientific matters, not everyone agreed with
Cvijić. F. Katzer, his name almost an anagram of karst, proposed that the solution of rocks was by water rising and
falling in natural siphons. A. Grund, as one would expect
from his name, proposed that groundwater was stagnant
below a base level, with the only circulation being descend-
ing rainwater. He claimed that karst formation led ulti-

mately to a roughly planar surface coincident with the level of stagnant water—level grund if you will.

Cvijić also held the essentially modern view that karst was composed of three zones: an upper one through which water percolated during storms but which was usually dry; a middle one that was also wet and dry but which was flooded for considerable periods; and a lower one that was always water filled and had permanent streams and reservoirs.

The details of how the subterranean rock became dissolved became a subject of debate. Each camp selected one of Cvijić's three zones as its home. Some held that solution only took place in zone one above the groundwater level as water percolated downward. The great American geomorphologist William Morris Davis held that most solution took place in zone three, below the water table, as water flowed deep within the earth. He thought that caves had formed in the past when the water table, the upper boundary of water-saturated soil or rock, was higher and that the land had been subsequently elevated and the caves exposed by river valleys and the water table lowered to expose the caves above the water table. The third group chose zone two as the place where cave formation took place.

The first idea, that solution above the water table was the major cave former, is fraught with difficulties. Downward percolation of water, dissolving limestone on its way down, certainly could account for many of the surface and near-surface features of karst, but to explain caves, the supporters of this theory called upon enlargement of cavities through abrasion of streams flowing downward through the passages created by solution. The problem is that most features of caves don't resemble abrasion features observed in surface streams.

Davis's idea, like most of his concepts, depends on a regular cycle of events, with cave formation at depth, followed by elevation of the land and lowering of the water table. He argued that almost all caves today are in a stage of deposition of material on the walls rather than solution of limestone, so that formation of caves above the water table was demonstrably not possible. Yet there are caves being formed today, as evidenced by changes observed from year to year in some caves.

We'll return to the third concept after a side trip into the chemistry of limestone and dolomite solution. I'll deal with the ideal case of pure calcite—calcium carbonate— because the principle is much the same for other carbonates such as dolomite.

Calcite is only slightly soluble in pure water, up to a maximum of about fourteen parts per million calcite. Natural waters are far from pure, however. Surface waters contain dissolved gases from the atmosphere, particularly carbon dioxide, which is highly soluble in water. Water in contact with ordinary atmospheric air contains about .015 percent carbon dioxide. That may not seem like a great deal, but it is enough to cause the water to be a weak acid and as such enable it to hold as much as ten times the amount of dissolved calcite as pure water. In a simplified view, water in contact with the atmosphere is weak carbonic acid, and calcite dissolves readily in acids.

Some natural waters contain far more carbon dioxide than surface waters and as a consequence are more efficient dissolvers of calcite. Near the ground, the carbon dioxide content of the atmosphere is higher than in the free atmosphere, and within soils the gas that fills the interstices between soil granules is vastly richer in carbon dioxide. As a consequence, water in the pores of soil contains a great deal more dissolved carbon dioxide and is therefore a more powerful solvent for calcite than ordinary water. Such is especially true in tropical and subtropical regions, and karsts are highly developed in such climates. Water in equilibrium with soil gases can contain dissolved calcium up to .07 percent, which in terms of calcite is about a hundred times that of pure water.

The upshot of this is that waters that have been in contact

with the atmosphere are efficient solvents for limestone. Surfaces of exposed limestone become pitted, deep cracks become etched, and water moves through the cracks and enlarges natural rock fractures as limestone is progressively dissolved away. Such a scenario would seem to support the idea that most solution takes place above the water table. However, most caves are extensive in a more or less horizontal direction, which suggests some relation to the water table.

In Davis's model, carbonated water percolates downward to the water table, then flows beneath the water, dissolving cave openings as it goes. However, as mentioned above, caves are generally extensive in the horizontal, and large portions are even relatively level. Below the water table water moves in curved paths that sweep deeply. If Davis's theory was correct, we would expect to find caves that swing in deep downward arcs, level out, then sweep back surfaceward again, and we don't find that pattern.

The third idea of cave formation, espoused by John Thrailkill of the University of Kentucky, suggests that dissolution of limestone to form caves takes place primarily in the uppermost part of the groundwater, just below the water table. He bases this conclusion on his study of Mammoth Cave in which he made detailed chemical studies of the surface and subsurface waters.

Thrailkill notes that water reaching the water table or even flowing through caves is richer in carbon dioxide than water in contact with the atmosphere. He attributes this to the cave atmosphere being richer in carbon dioxide because of soil gases mixing with the cave air and to the subsurface waters reaching the water table more rapidly than they could react fully with calcite in the overlying rocks.

Thus, the downward-percolating water would dissolve a certain amount of limestone on its way down, but because the solution reaction is a slow one, it would still retain some capacity to dissolve even when it reached the water table or a subterranean stream. Thrailkill proposes that water movement in the uppermost portion of the groundwater is more or less parallel to the groundwater surface. Thus, caves would be etched out along that boundary layer of moving water. His concept fits well with the geography of Mammoth Cave and surrounding features.

There is one additional aspect of calcite solution in carbonated water that fits very well with solution of limestone below the water table, especially in the uppermost zone of mixing of groundwater with downward-percolating water.

We know that the solubility of calcite in water increases as the carbon-dioxide content of the water increases. That relation isn't proportional, however. What I mean by that is that if you double the amount of carbon dioxide in the water, you don't just double the solubility of calcite in the water. The relation is such that increases in carbon dioxide in the water have less and less effect on calcite solubility as the total content of carbon dioxide increases.

This relationship results in a situation that seems contrary to common sense at first. A solution that contains the maximum solid it can hold dissolved is said to be saturated in that solid. Suppose we had two different saturated solutions of calcite in carbonated water, water with two different levels of dissolved carbon dioxide. If we mixed these two solutions together, we would then have a single saturated solution. Right? Wrong.

Because of the relationship between calcite solubility and dissolved carbon dioxide, the intermediate mixture between any two saturated solutions can dissolve more calcite. It is said to be undersaturated. In a more general way, mixing any carbonated water with any other water, of either higher or lower carbonation, will increase its capacity for dissolving limestone. Although it sounds like two plus two gives more than four, it is nevertheless true.

Thus, in the upper part of the groundwater, mixing of downward-percolating water increases the dissolution capacity of that upper layer, and solution to form caves is a probable event. It matters not whether the water from above has dissolved all of the limestone it can carry on its downward trip and is saturated or whether it moved rapidly and is not carrying a full load of dissolved calcite. Either way, the new mixture will be able to dissolve more limestone.

Therefore, one would expect extensive horizontal networks of caves to form at levels where the water table was stable for long periods. If the table stood at different levels during different seasons, then a cave system might develop at each level, and so forth. Thrailkill's idea is much strengthened by the peculiar behavior of calcite solutions in carbonated water.

The dissolving properties of mixed waters account for some otherwise unexplainable properties of caves. Where two fractures meet in caves, there is often a large bell-shaped room formed. The room probably formed because two different solutions met and mixed at the juncture of the two fractures. Commonly, these large "rooms" become smaller downstream, away from the intersection of the fractures. This is an expression of the mixed water losing its capacity to dissolve limestone as it flows away from the region of mixing. Some very large cavities are fed by small, tubular openings. Such cavities must represent mixing of saturated waters from the small openings to form a solution capable of dissolving out the large chamber.

As far as a general theory of cave formation goes, probably all three of the proposed mechanisms contribute to the formation of any given cave. Obviously a great deal of solution takes place above the water table, and no doubt there is solution of limestone by undersaturated water moving deep below the water table, as envisaged by Davis and later by the controversial J Harlan Bretz of the University of Chicago. Furthermore, there is ample evidence of enlarging of caves by abrasion.

In a recent paper USGS geologist Warren Wood describes

measurements in west Texas that show carbon dioxide content increasing with depth in the zone above the water table. He explains this puzzling information by proposing that there are aerobic—oxygen using—bacteria which make their living by oxidizing organic matter at depth. His model satisfactorily explains why caves enlarge with depth rather than the reverse because the limestone-dissolving carbonic acid is produced at depth by solution of locally-produced carbon dioxide in groundwater.

Getting back to the so-called cave "formations" that the books show and the tourists want to see, we might ask how they form. The classic stalactites and curtainlike sheets of rock hanging from the ceiling and stalagmites rising majestically from the floor are the tourists' favorites. Those features are composed of layers of calcite built one on the other. Each stalactite is like a series of cones nested one inside the other, with the most recent layer on the outside. A standard explanation for all of these features is that calcite-laden water percolating from above runs slowly down the stalactite or curtain or drips onto the stalagmite and the calcite is left behind when the water evaporates in the atmosphere of the cave.

Such a theory presupposes that the water can evaporate. If you have ever been in a cave with active deposition of cave formations, you will have noticed that everything is wet. If you were to measure the humidity of the air, you would find that it was 100 percent. In other words, it is saturated with water and can contain no more. Therefore, the water dripping down a stalactite couldn't possibly evaporate.

How, then, is the calcite deposited? Remember that the water percolating from above has passed through a soil zone and become enriched in carbon dioxide on its way down. Thus enriched, it is able to dissolve large amounts of calcite on its trip to the cave. Once reaching the cave atmosphere, the dripping water encounters air with far less carbon dioxide in it than the soil air above. When this happens, carbon dioxide begins to leave the water for the air to achieve a balance under the new conditions. As a result, the solvent capacity of the water is greatly reduced, and some calcite must deposit on the cave formations. No evaporation need take place, only transfer of carbon dioxide from the water to the air.

Deposition of calcite by this mechanism is reasonably rapid in geologic terms. I visited a cave in California that was a commercially developed cave in the 1860s and 1870s. There carefully drawn on the wall in pencil was the name Ulysses S. Grant and the names of the party accompanying him. The whole wall was a directory of well-known and not so well-known people who had visited the cave in its heyday. One would be tempted to think that the names, at least Grant's, were fakes, but still their antiquity was supported by the fact that they were covered by a quarter inch of clear calcite.

Many caves have portions with walls covered by sparkling crystals of calcite rather than the layered deposits so typical of stalactites and stalagmites. Such crystals must have formed out of solution below the water table by analogy with other such crystals. There are a number of possibilities, but the basic mechanism must include a chamber filled with water. Furthermore, the situation must be such that new water is not added constantly, because the mixing effect would cause solution, not deposition of crystals. Some mechanism that reduces the solubility of the calcite must be at work. There are two likely possibilities. First, the chamber could be vented to the outside through cracks and fractures that allowed the carbon dioxide to escape. Alternately, the water might have warmed up, driving the carbon dioxide out of solution. Cold water contains more carbon dioxide than warm, so warming causes a diminishing of its solvent capacity for calcite.

If you have visited a wild cave or have strayed off the

path of a developed one, you'll have noticed that there is
soft clay on parts of the floors, sometimes in big accumulations. This clay is what's left after the limestone or dolomite
is dissolved. It is very fine grained and makes a mess of your
clothes. It is also very slippery, and dangerous in some
situations. Some chambers in caves show evidence of having
been filled by transported clay at times in their history.

Caves are beloved by vertebrate paleontologists and archaeologists. They provide shelter from the elements that
has preserved paintings on the walls, feces on the floors,
marks from campfire smoke, and a huge number of fossils
of man as well as other vertebrates. Just as caves collapse
on modern spelunkers now and then, they did so in the
past. In one cave in Africa, elephants were often killed and
buried when they entered the cave to eat salts crusting the
ceiling, and dislodged rock collapsed in the process. C. K.
Brain of the Transvaal Museum has spent much of his life
exploring caves in South Africa for remains of the ancestors
and distant cousins of modern man. Even in regions where
real caves are not present, animal remains have been preserved in sinkholes and deep fractures.

Some karst has been buried in the past, and we now find
exposed what is loosely called paleokarst. Limestone layers
in some areas show exhumed sinks, fissures, caves, and the
like, often filled with overlying sediment from the layers
above. The openings in the karst can also preserve remnants
of rocks that were stripped off the old surface by erosion in
the distant past. Such preserved bits of rock are our only
evidence in an otherwise blank page in geologic history in
some regions.

Some of you may have associated the formation of karst
with acid rain, and you're right. Normal rain is acidic from
the carbon dioxide dissolved in it and becomes more so from
the additional carbon dioxide in soil as well as various organic acids, loosely called humic acids, arising from decay-
ing organic matter. Man's additional contribution to the
acidity of rain comes from oxides of sulfur and nitrogen

that add to the acid content of rain in some regions, mainly from smelting of ores and burning of fuels.

You have probably inferred from the foregoing that regions with plenty of limestones, dolomites, and carbonate rich rocks of other types suffer few adverse environmental effects from acid rain because its acid content is quickly neutralized by reaction with calcite or other carbonate minerals. In some regions, acid rain is even beneficial agriculturally because sulfur is added to the soil when sulfuric and sulfurous acids react with soil carbonates.

In geologic terranes composed of noncarbonate rocks, the situation is quite different, and the acids can accumulate in lakes, marshes, and soils in the absence of reactive minerals. Because of the distribution of rocks in North America, adverse effects from acid rain are seen primarily in the Northeast, in Canada, and in some of the high mountains of the Pacific states, places where carbonate-rich rocks are not prevalent. Geology accidentally enters into politics in this case because regional political leanings have a rough correlation with the degree of the acid-rain problem. The conservative heartland is a region with plenty of acid buffering, and the liberal Northeast and northern tier get the brunt of the problem. So by virtue of rock types, as well as other factors, the acid-rain issue is one of right versus left. It's a strange world.

Lastly, in the realm of strange worlds, most of us have seen Chinese paintings of a mystical-looking land with towering, steep-sided hills rising above a flat plain. I imagine that you have, as I once did, equated those paintings with the elaborately artificial Japanese pictures of surf and waves. The Japanese pictures are indeed exaggerations, but the Chinese ones are not. The region depicted is in southern China, mostly in Kweichow and Kwangsi provinces, up the Pearl River from Canton and extending into neighboring Vietnam. The Chinese karst is more karsty than the real thing, with towers and cones hundreds of feet high developed in a layer of limestone over a half mile thick. More-

over, the steep-sided hills are pierced by several systems of
caves at different levels, many of which are decorated with
spectacular secondary deposits. One wonders what a vocabulary the Chinese must have to describe their superkarst.
The mind reels.

CHAPTER THIRTEEN

Where the Buffalo Roam

Most people today are not antagonistic to the concept that there were once living organisms on the earth that are no longer extant. Extinction is accepted as part of the history of life. Easy acceptance of that concept was not always the case. Even as late as the end of the eighteenth century there was a general belief that the combination of animals and plants created by God was a perfectly balanced one and that extinction not only implied that the deity had made an error in the original creation but that removal of a single species would destroy the complex interworkings among all the organisms and the whole biological system would collapse in disorganization.

Arguments in favor of extinction as a natural process were largely based on the discovery of fossils of small shelled invertebrates, and the antiextinctionists countered them by pointing out that new discoveries of previously unknown organisms were being made all the time and that it was just a matter of future discovery to prove that the supposed extinct species still lived somewhere on the earth. The great biologist Baron George Cuvier was a firm believer in extinction, and he settled the disagreement by basing his arguments on large mammals, animals so large that they could not very well be hiding undiscovered in some remote corner of the world. Cuvier's strategy succeeded for the most part, although today there are still people obtaining funding to look for dinosaurs in African swamps and monsters in northern lakes. One suspects that much of the funding comes from today's creationists.

Cuvier's demonstration that extinction did really occur was quickly reconciled with religion by accepting the view that the creation was so miraculous that the whole, complex system still worked even when elements were plucked from it.

The two creationist viewpoints are not that dissimilar from modern ideas about ecological niches. One camp holds that all niches in a given region must be filled by organisms that utilize the space and resources of the niches. Another group believes that niches can remain unoccupied without disturbance of the whole ecosystem—the later creationist viewpoint.

As to why some animals became extinct and others did not, there were varied opinions. Darwin was conservative in his views on the matter, although he expressed the idea that we should not be any more puzzled that an animal was extinct than that a living species was rare. He commented on the question in *The Origin of Species* (1859) as follows:

> Whenever we can precisely say why this species is more abundant in individuals than that; why this species and not another can be naturalized in a given country; then, and not till then, we may justly feel surprise why we cannot account for the extinction of any particular species or group of species.

It was clear to Darwin and many of his contemporaries that many organisms had become extinct, but the reasons were not so clear. Cuvier and the English geologist William Buckland espoused catastrophic death from floods. Later, Agassiz put the blame on glaciers for equally catastrophic removal of extinct forms, confronting Charles Lyell's gradualistic views. Through the years the catastrophists lost ground to the gradualists as Lyell's uniformitarianism doctrine took a firm hold on the thinking of earth scientists.

Whatever the mechanisms or timing of extinctions, it became obvious that there had been many episodes of extinction in earth history, and indeed it seemed that extinction was the normal and usual fate of any given species. In addition, evidence was clear for several intervals in earth history during which many lines became extinct at about the same time, the best known of which is probably the demise of the dinosaurs at the end of the Cretaceous Period, about sixty-five million years ago.

The end of the dinosaurs was mirrored by many other animal lines at about the same time, and one modern view is that the extinctions were caused by catastrophic impact of an extraterrestrial object and its ancillary effects. That explanation takes us back to catastrophism with a new twist, and while there is considerable enthusiasm, one might even say bandwagonism, for that explanation, there are many serious scientists, myself included, who are more than a little skeptical. However, that is another story.

The other well-known extinction pulse was at the end of the last ice age, the end of the Pleistocene Epoch and the beginning of the Holocene, or present, Epoch about ten thousand years ago. This extinction event, commonly called the Pleistocene extinction or Quaternary extinction, formed much of Cuvier's evidence as well as having influenced Darwin's thinking decades later, for Darwin saw abundant evidence in the Americas of geologically recently extinct animals of great variety.

The Pleistocene extinctions are additionally of interest because they overlap in time with the appearance of *Homo sapiens* on the scene. Furthermore, the geography of the world has changed little since the Pleistocene so that one can relate more directly with what sort of animals walked North America or Europe some several thousands of years ago than with the flora and fauna of tens or hundreds of million years past. It is almost infinitely fascinating to imagine the Appalachians inhabited by lions, cheetahs, saber-toothed tigers, musk ox, tapirs, caribou, horses, ground sloths, mastodons, mammoths, dire wolves, and huge bears as well as more familiar animals such as deer, elk, coyotes, skunks, and badgers.

One might think, too, that the Pleistocene extinctions could provide a valuable model for scientists to use in explaining more ancient extinctions, because the geologic record of the Pleistocene and Holocene Epochs is so much more complete than that of more distant times. Also, radiocarbon dating can provide age determinations accurate to as little as one hundred years under ideal circumstances, so the relative age of events in the record can be readily determined. Alas, we shall see that this is not the case. In fact, the Pleistocene extinctions tell us at least as much about science and scientists as they do about the death of ancient animals.

As I've said, floods and glaciers were called upon as agents of extinction in the eighteenth and nineteenth centuries. Many other ideas were put forward in subsequent years, but standing out among them were extinction caused by climatic change and extinction caused by activities of man. At first, climatic changes were accepted as the most reasonable cause. The extinctions had occurred at the end of the last glacial episode, when climates must have undergone profound changes all over the world, and particularly in the Northern Hemisphere, where much of the evidence had been observed. The influence of man was recognized as important but was not generally accepted as sufficient in itself to cause extinction.

I'll return to the possible causes, but first a look at some of the evidence. I'll restrict my comments mostly to North America, because the sequence and timing of events and probably the causes of the events are different for the different continents. In any case, North America will provide more than enough confusion and paradox all by itself.

To begin with, there is no doubt that a lot of animal lines became extinct at the end of the Pleistocene Epoch, but was there really a Pleistocene extinction event? Was the late Pleistocene a unique event, or was it just one episode in a larger series of extinction?

If we look at the last three hundred million years or so of earth history, we find that there has been a succession of four-footed animal groups, each of which expanded in diversity and numbers to the point where romantics would say they "ruled the earth" and each of which went into a decline and died out over a period of several million or tens of millions of years. Are mammals one of these groups? Have the mammals started to decline in importance, or are they still rulers?

According to my old colleague at Wyoming, Jay Lille-graven, mammals reached a peak of diversity in the early Miocene Epoch, about twenty million years ago. At that time, the proportion of large mammals was on the increase, a sign of maturity, or maybe even an over-the-hill stage. By twelve to fifteen million years ago, in North America there was an increase in diversity of hooved animals such as horses, pronghorns, and camels, which probably represented adaptation to increased areas of open land at the expense of forests rather than a vigorous expansion of mammals in general.

By the late Miocene Epoch, about nine million years ago, mammals were starting a slide, with the extinction of numerous very large forms. By four million years ago, peccaries, horses, rhinos, pronghorns, and other mixed feeders and grazers were sharply reduced. By two million years ago, diversity of all groups was greatly reduced. Extinctions continued to the end of the Pleistocene Epoch. At present, diversity among herbivores is greatest among rodents, with large mammals very much in the minority as far as numbers of genera or species is concerned.

Does this mean that the Pleistocene extinction was just one episode in a gradual decline of mammals? Unfortunately, the answer is yes and no. If the Pleistocene extinction was a separate event and not just part of the overall decline in mammal diversity, then it should be possible to demonstrate from the fossil record that an unusually large number of genera or species died out at that time. The trouble is that the time resolution is good for the end of the Pleistocene Epoch but not as good for older parts of the Cenozoic Era. A large number of forms became extinct during the interval from six to four and a half million years ago, but we have insufficient resolution to know whether they vanished gradually over a million and a half years or whether they all dropped out abruptly over a few thousand or tens of thousands of years. If the extinctions took place in thousands of years, then that extinction event would greatly overshadow the one at the end of the Pleistocene Epoch. It is because of the nature of the geologic record that paleontologists will never be able to improve the accuracy of their data from five million years ago to the level of ten thousand years ago. Thus, our answer is that *maybe* the Pleistocene extinction was a unique event, or perhaps it was just the end of a slide that started twenty million years ago. Throughout the Cenozoic Era there is evidence that extinctions were more common at the end of glacial episodes, so the Pleistocene extinction may be just one of many—in a climatic sense as well as in a biologic one.

Perhaps it doesn't really matter whether or not the Pleistocene extinctions were part of a bigger decline or not. We do know that lions with manes no longer lie in the sun in Pennsylvania and great, lumbering mammoths no longer dominate the skyline of Nebraska. Whether or not their demise was trendy, they are gone, and it is interesting to speculate on what caused their death, or at least helped them along a possibly predestined path.

The question of cause has become simplified into an either/or situation. Either man did it or climate did it. Other possible causes have been forgotten in the face of the man-versus-climate controversy. The main thread of the story began in the 1950s when Paul Martin of the University of Arizona concluded from his studies of pollen in Arizona that climatic change didn't quite jibe with the time of extinction of mammals in the region. He also was impressed by the apparent hunting skills of the Clovis early man that he inferred from archaeological digs. He decided that man had caused the Pleistocene extinctions, not an idea new to him, for such a scenario had been suggested in the nineteenth century by a number of leading scientists, but Martin pursued the idea vigorously.

Science moves ahead by individual scientists getting ideas and then testing them to see if the idea stands up to the evidence. Naturally there is an element of bias in a person testing a pet theory, but we all try to be as objective as we can. The other side of the coin is that a new concept is very exciting to the conceiver, and he or she makes all possible haste to spread the word by talking with colleagues, giving lectures to peer groups, and writing papers for the scientific journals. All of that dissemination of the new idea is part of the system whereby a new idea is constantly challenged by other ideas and additional evidence.

In the long view, if a concept survives numerous tests and challenges, it may become accepted by a consensus within the scientific community. That is not to say that it remains accepted forever, but it becomes part of the lore of the science for at least a time. If an idea survives tests, it becomes less and less testable and gathers strength or resilience against detractors.

One factor that enters in is the personal traits of the person or persons proposing a new idea. Some are shy and don't talk or write about their ideas either very much or very effectively. Others are charismatic speakers and talented writers, and they not only get their ideas out in a skillful manner, but they are able to defend against challenges by virtue of their communication skills.

Martin was, and is, a prolific writer and a convincing speaker—an eloquent spokesman for his ideas. He told his story widely and gained many adherents. As time went on, the concept that man had caused the Pleistocene extinctions became a hard theory to fight. Martin saw to it that the concept was reinforced over and over again.

Martin's concept involved more than just man the hunter killing all of the big game, for indeed it did seem that the extinctions were mostly extinctions of large animals such as might be attractive game animals to a skilled hunter armed with a spear or other missile. Martin suggested that the extinction in North America took place in a sweeping wave that he termed the *blitzkrieg* in a chilling parallel to the overrunning of Europe by Hitler's armies in the early days of World War II.

As far as can be told, man entered North America from Asia by moving across what is now the Bering Straits, through Alaska, and down an ice-free corridor that ended near the present site of Edmonton, Alberta. Martin suggested that man spread out from that point in an arcuate wave, killing as the wave moved forward. His concept was that the newly arrived hunters would effectively kill off all the desirable animals, then move on, leaving a population behind that was so decimated that the hunted species died off altogether. He assumed that the well-fed Indians would have multiplied rapidly with the abundant resources available and the semicircular wave of advance would have remained coherent as it swept southward. He assumed a reasonable rate of advance of about 30 miles a year, which meant that all of North America would have been occupied by man and swept clean of many large mammals in just a few hundred years.

Martin's blitzkrieg idea has a dramatic appeal that helped popularize it. The alternate human-based hypothesis of man expanding over the region and just hunting as needed wasn't nearly as exciting. In any case, man had done the latter in Europe without extinctions quite as dramatic as those in North America. The blitzkrieg concept also had one other advantage. It avoided one otherwise fatal test, the lack of association of human and hunted animal remains in archaeological sites.

The only animal remains that have been found with human associations are mammoths, and later, bison. Yet Martin's hypothesis called for man to have hunted numerous species to extinction. Where was the evidence? Ah, Martin countered; the wave of hunter-gatherers sweeping through the countryside simply didn't remain in one place long enough to leave artifacts to be discovered, and by the time they did form more permanent dwelling sites, the animals were already extinct. In fact, argued Martin, the lack of association of hunted animal fossils with human artifacts was positive evidence *in favor* of the blitzkrieg idea.

As you can see, the blitzkrieg is a difficult concept to overturn. Some critics call it an untestable, and therefore an inadequate, concept. Martin states that the absence of other evidence was a test that it survived. He did set up one test that has not been successfully used against the idea. He argued that radiocarbon dating showed that the extinctions took place about eleven thousand to twelve thousand years ago. Therefore, he considered that any solid evidence for man's entry into North America prior to that time would overturn his idea. To date there has been no such evidence found that all agree upon. There is a recent report of an elephant-hunting (mammoths and mastodons) culture in northern Venezuela that existed thirteen thousand, or even as much as sixteen thousand, years ago. Radiocarbon dates on kills associated with stone weapon points is well documented. The points are not those of Clovis man. If the dates hold up to challenges and confirmations, then the blitzkrieg concept is dead, because any humans in South America would be presumed to have gotten there via North America. Martin's theory, for it has nearly attained that status for many scientists, is based on timing, which is in turn based on stratigraphy, the relation of one rock unit to another in time, and on radiometric dating. If a piece of evidence is out of place in the time sequence, the theory may crumble.

The alternate explanation for the Pleistocene extinctions is climatic change and all of the various environmental changes and effects on the biota that a climatic change would cause. Is there evidence of climatic change? Indeed there is, and it was climatic change that Paul Martin was investigating by looking at fossil pollens in Arizona. He concluded that Arizona climates hadn't changed that much and went on to develop his man-the-destroyer ideas. But Arizona isn't the world, and the climate camp has a great deal of evidence to support climatically caused extinctions.

In the United States, great changes took place at the end of the Pleistocene Epoch. There had been a great belt of forested parkland with primarily spruce trees that extended from Wyoming to the Atlantic coastal plain. It was an ecologically diverse habitat that offered a great variety of niches to a rich fauna that included elephants, horses, bison, musk ox, tapirs, ground sloths, elk and deer, caribou, and many less familiar animals. At the end of the Pleistocene that system collapsed, with mixed hardwoods and pines replacing the parklands in the East and grasslands taking over in the West.

In the East, the fauna that survived was much less varied, with deer and their kindred the only important browser-grazer in a canopied forest that provided little food for large herbivores. In the West, bison and the modern prong-horn, formerly rare animals, greatly increased in numbers, taking advantage of a relatively uniform new environment that was highly favorable to their needs in contrast to the previous diverse parkland that favored a mixed and varied fauna not unlike that in East Africa today. The change in both East and West resulted from a highly varied environment that supported complex assemblages of species to more uniform settings that were unsuitable for most of the old residents but highly suitable for a few. Such changes are well documented for many parts of North America, and those who favor a climatic cause for the extinctions cite them as evidence. Those favoring climatic change over man's influence have also invoked drought, young born out of season, cold weather, and decline in food resources, or combinations of those factors, as causal agents.

Dale Guthrie, a University of Alaska zoologist, has put together a coherent model that challenges the Martin overkill theory with a vast array of data. His model proposes that climatic changes in seasonal regimes decreased diversity and increased zonation of plant communities, causing changes in antiherbivore traits of plants. That change in the plant community caused a shorter, less diverse growing season for hooved animals as well as a reduction in both quantity and quality of resources for many large species. The restrictions in resources decreased local faunal diversity, body size, and ranges and resulted in many extinctions.

Guthrie argues that climatic changes throughout the Cenozoic Era tended to general cooling and increased seasonality and a shortening of the growing season for plants. He envisions the opening of an extensive woodland cover and the increase in shrubs and herbs at the expense of trees. Such a change increased the variety of food resources and resulted in the development of the richly varied mammalian fauna of the Miocene and Pliocene Epochs. As the trend to seasonality continued, the complex faunas diminished, but some elements such as mammoths, bison, and horses flourished and grew large but then experienced a decline in body size in the Pleistocene Epoch.

Guthrie speaks of the changes in plant communities in terms of a change from plaids to stripes. His research indicates that the Pleistocene vegetation was one that was varied on a local scale in a patchy or plaid way, with small, diverse plant communities growing side by side. He attributes this arrangement to long and varied growing seasons during the glacial episodes. At the change to the Holocene Epoch, Guthrie hypothesizes shorter growing seasons with less variable climate. That resulted in the simplification of

plant communities, because the plants that were best ad-
justed to the new, stable conditions could compete better
and form a specialized plant stand that was adapted to a
particular set of conditions. The new communities formed
stripes such as zones related to elevation or latitude.

Dwarfing and reduction of "social organs" such as horns,
antlers, and the like reflected a diminution in the available
food resources for the hooved mammals. Large size and the
size of social organs are indications of healthy, robust populations with adequate resources. With a shorter growing
season, resources were directed more to mere survival.

Some species simply adapted better to the new simplified
flora of the Holocene. Bison, pronghorns, musk ox, and
others thrived on the grasses that appeared in abundance.
Elk, some deer, and moose prospered on a diet of leaves
and twigs by selective feeding. Guthrie suggests that the
deer and their kin helped to eliminate the mammoth by
eating only the nutritious tips of branches in winter. With
the tips gone, the mammoth, which ate whole twigs, was
left with a diet that did not meet its minimum nutritional
needs.

In addition, plants have various defenses against preda-
tion from herbivores. Grasses contain silica that wears down
teeth, but long, growing teeth counter the wearing effect.
Other plants contain toxic substances. In a mixed plant
community mammals can vary their diet among various
species to reduce concentrations of toxins; not so in more
limited assemblages.

The arrangement of the digestive system also affects what
a mammal can eat. Ruminants such as bison or pronghorn
have several advantages over one-stomached animals such
as horses, tapirs, and elephants. For one thing the bacterial
breakdown of feed in the rumen detoxifies most plant toxins.
For another, nitrogen is recycled in the ruminants so that
the rumen bacteria are kept healthy and growing even in
a shortage of quality feed. The one-stomached mammals on
the other hand cannot detoxify plants in their digestive

system; in fact, the toxins are absorbed higher in their tract than the nutrients. They do have a seeming advantage over ruminants in that they can simply eat more of lower-quality food to obtain nutrients, whereas the ruminants must have sufficient protein in the feed to keep the rumen flora active.

The downfall of the one-stomached mammals may have been partly a result of competition such as that of the deer kindred with the mammoths or that of bison and pronghorn versus the horses and camels, but it appears that some aspects of breeding and nutrition of the young played a role, as well. The mammals that became extinct had long gestation periods and relatively low milk protein. In a seasonal climate, animals with gestation periods of about a year would have to breed in the spring in order to birth in the following spring, when feed conditions were good for both lactation of the female and vegetation feeding by the young. Spring breeding could be a failure if it followed a difficult winter with restricted feed, which would have resulted in greatly reduced fertility. The ruminants with short gestation periods breed in the fall after a season of abundant feed and birth in the spring when conditions are favorable for the young in addition to having much higher levels of protein in their milk. Thus, the timing of reproductive activity probably loomed large in favoring the survivors of the Pleistocene-Holocene change in climate.

I have mentioned mostly herbivorous animals, but many carnivores died out, as well. For the most part, it appears that the carnivores that became extinct were specialists whose favorite prey became extinct. A tale of specialists is told by fossils found in Friesenhahn Cave, which is about thirty-five miles north of San Antonio, Texas. The cave contains numerous skeletons of the scimitar cat (*Homotherium serum*), including juveniles, indicating that the cave was used as a den. Also, there are numerous skeletons, but more significant, milk molars of Jefferson's mammoth (441 milk molars and only 14 adult teeth) and milk molars of mastodons. It appears that the great cats preyed almost exclusively on calves of mammoths and mastodons and carried the kill back to the cave. One can imagine that it was quite a trick for even a large cat to avoid getting killed by a protective mother mammoth while picking off its youngster. With the demise of the "elephants," which the cats helped by killing the young, the cats became extinct, as well.

Guthrie proposes that the entry of man into North America was brought about by climatic changes, which resulted in alterations to the Arctic environment. He reconstructs the glacial Arctic as a cold, windy, treeless, and virtually snowless plain in Alaska and neighboring Siberia. Around twelve thousand years ago the winter snows became deeper, and winds diminished. Shrub lands and woodlands began to colonize at a rapid rate. The more habitable winter, combined with wood for tools and cooking, may well have allowed man to make the trip to North America just as the same climatic changes were causing extinctions there. Guthrie argues that the colonization by man and the extinctions were both caused by climatic change and are only coincidentally related to one another.

Scientists have also suggested that while the diversity of mammals, especially large mammals, decreased through the Pleistocene extinctions, the total biomass of large mammals may have remained the same or even increased. A complex environment changed to one of vast regions of simpler characteristics, and the mammal residents did the same, with many taxonomic groups with small numbers of individuals giving way to a few groups with large populations.

Where do we stand, then, in the argument between Martin and his followers and the supporters of the equally eloquent Guthrie? Two authors have compared the controversy to "Who Killed Cock Robin?" The question is Do we have sufficient evidence to judge the merits of the case? Certainly there is lots of evidence, but each camp uses it as it sees fit.

If we accept Guthrie's view that the change at the Pleistocene-Holocene boundary was unprecedented in the

Cenozoic Era and that the climatic changes alone were more than sufficient to account for faunal changes that occurred, then we must sort out the role of man. It is interesting to note that among the large mammals that survived into the Holocene, the pronghorn is the only one that didn't have long association with man in Europe. American moose, caribou, bear, bison, and deer have their analogues (and ancestors) in Europe. In fact, the pronghorn is the only native North American large mammal that survived the extinction. It is interesting, too, that the surviving pronghorn was a relatively rare mammal prior to the extinction, and many of its close relations died out.

The large mammals that survived in North America are species that seem to thrive in the presence of man. Deer and their kin are practically a nuisance in many populated areas. Pronghorns are absurdly abundant in Wyoming. Coyotes are omnipresent. Black bears are overrunning some regions. If man the hunter is to be blamed for extinction of some species, then he must be credited as man the farmer-rancher, man the roadside ditch maker, and man the town builder for creating highly favorable environments for some species. The opossum and the raccoon are now common through much of the United States rather than restricted to the Southeast. Armadillos threaten to take over Texas and have invaded as far north as Nebraska. We see a remarkable symbiosis among man and a host of mammals. Have the activities of man tended to cancel some of the effects of climate? Probably so. Even the bison seems to be making a comeback from the hide and tongue hunters of a century and more ago as ranchers find that they are more successful inhabitants of the plains than cattle.

Insofar as solving "Who Killed Cock Robin?" we are probably no closer to a verdict than we were in the nineteenth century. To be sure, we have lots more evidence, but we also have a hung jury. Mike Voorhies of the University of Nebraska suggested to me that what is needed is a really detailed study of pollen samples from the earlier glacial and interglacial stages. If the Pleistocene-Holocene change was really a more severe one than previous passages from glacial to interglacial, then perhaps the climate concept gains strength.

The dwarfing of many animals prior to their extinction suggests to me that a gradual process was coming to an end, not that a sudden effect was caused by climate or man. Some argue that the dwarfing resulted from selective hunting of large individuals by man. Thus, the claim is made, small-sized animals are left to reproduce the race, and size diminishes. This sort of process certainly takes place on farms with domestic animals, but I find it a bit much to imagine that hunting would cause such changes. Hunters have sought large buck deer for many years without causing dwarfing of our native whitetails or mule deer.

Any hypothesis that seeks to explain the Pleistocene extinction in North America must take into account both man and climate. It also must account for the fact that animals migrated both to and from North America. The canid dogs were exclusively North American until the mid-Pleistocene when they went to Asia. Camels and horses also took that eastward trip. The only large and medium-sized native animals that survived were the pronghorn, canids, badgers, and some cats. There were numerous South American imports in North America in the Pleistocene, but the only ones left are the porcupine and the armadillo. All of the other survivors are Eurasian imports that replaced the extinct animals. Those animals either displaced the competition or occupied a void created by the death of potential competition. Either way, the Eurasians were preadapted to the environments and slipped into them easily. The Eurasian imports were also preadapted to man by long association and survival. As Mike Voorhies observed to me once, we should look at the animals that survived, not those that became extinct.

I would close by saying something like time will tell, but past history suggests otherwise. Maybe pollen studies or more discoveries of old human sites will provide guidance, or perhaps this is a debate that will never conclude. After all, testing one another's views is what science is all about, anyway, and nothing is ever really proved, only strongly supported by both evidence and believers.

CHAPTER FOURTEEN

Elysian Fields

The summer after I graduated from Berkeley, I was the teaching assistant for the summer field course then taught by Professor N. L. Taliaferro, a salty veteran of a lifetime of field seasons. Taliaferro was a confusing mystery to newly arrived students at Berkeley, because while they saw his name in the catalog and listed on a mailbox, they had also heard of a Dr. Tolliver and someone nicknamed Tucky, all of whom seemed to have common interests and specialties. Of course all three were the same person, because Taliaferro was from one of those English families that intentionally disregard phonetics when pronouncing the family name, so Taliaferro becomes a phonetic Tolliver just as Chumlabaugh becomes Chumly. Taliaferro's background on the west side of the Atlantic was Kentucky, hence the nickname.

I, like so many students, had been attracted to geology partly because of the field aspect of the science. I had been in field courses with Taliaferro and several other Berkeley faculty and looked forward to being a staff member, however lowly, and doing more work in the field. Field geology and geologic maps are the underpinning of geology for they provide us with the basic framework around which all other studies are built. A geologic map provides the context for all other examinations of a given part of the earth. A map is an interpretation, not a fact, but it is the starting point for all geologic research—even for earth scientists who never leave the laboratory.

After a scorching day in the field in the Sierra Nevada foothills, the staff members, including Chuck Higgins of the California Davis campus as well as Tucky and me, would meet at our camp, a dry pasture dotted with oaks and poison-oak bushes of antediluvian size. After a shower in a stall without walls—field camp was an all-male bastion in those days—the three of us would dress in the cleanest clothes we had and drive to a cafe in a nearby town for dinner.

Tucky was a man who used colorful language to say the least, and our meal was generally fairly lively, with conversation and anecdotes punctuated by the boss, who would pull at his little mustache and utter carefully and slowly pronounced profanities out of the side of his mouth. I found out what one of our regular waitresses thought about us when a student hailed us on the street in Angel's Camp one evening. We went to the usual cafe, and the waitress asked the student if he'd found the professors. He responded that he had and that we were they. The waitress reared back with her hands on her hips and said, "Those guys are professors?"

Her comment reflects a characteristic of field geologists that has remained unchanged almost from the inception of the science. Field geologists do a lot of walking, climbing fences, fording creeks, running from domestic animals, and other activities that take their toll on personal appearance. Even freshly washed clothes, an uncommon garb, are seldom ironed and usually bear numerous stains and battle scars. The geologist is invariably sunburned and thirsty, and in situations where showers are a rarity, is commonly sweaty and dirty, as well. It was obvious that

the Mother Lode country waitress couldn't imagine any
of us, especially Tucky, in proper dress, addressing a class
or gathering of scholars.

In Victorian times the same problem is said to have
existed, and the Geological Survey of Great Britain began
a policy of requiring its field men to dress as proper gentle-
men. The edict had two results. First, the top-hatted and
swallowtailed scientists proved to look very silly clambering over outcrops and whacking at them with hammers.
Second, the well-dressed geologists lost all their rapport
with the common country folk and were thus deprived of a
great deal of valuable information about the lay of the
land and its rocks. The Brits quit the fancy dress for more
practical clothing for the most part, and Americans have
always favored simple field duds, with rare exceptions. I
do recall a field trip with Harvard's Marland Billings
during which he wore a pinstriped suit, black topcoat, and
highly polished black shoes, but his garb wasn't the norm
any more than that of one USGS geologist, whose name I
won't reveal, who wore a jock strap and a pair of pearl-
handled .45 revolvers on his Arizona sojourns.

I mention all of this because field geologists are often
thought of as rough, uncultured individuals—a far cry from
a real scientist. Appearances can be very deceiving, for the
best field geologists are among the most artful practitioners
of the scientific method. They deal with the most complex
system of all the sciences with the goal of unraveling the
past from great experiments already completed for them.
They must accept the data that are present, and make
scientific sense out of it—no simple task.

In addition to looking very unlike a waitress's image of a
professor and using a richly decorated style of language,
Tucky was also a consummate field geologist. He had had a
lung removed because of cancer, so he was running on
halved air capacity, which, together with being in his
middle sixties, slowed him down a bit. I went on one trip
with him as a visitor, so that, unlike the students, I could

observe without the need to take notes or record observations on a map. Although Tucky walked very slowly, the students, healthy college juniors and seniors, were hard-pressed to keep up with him. I watched the puzzling situation for a while and finally realized what Tucky was doing. He would arrive at an outcropping of rock, look it over, perhaps take a sample or a measurement, make a mark on his map, glance around, and head for another outcrop. The students did the same things superficially, yet they were constantly scratching their heads, looking around, asking one another questions, and then, seeing Taliaferro already thirty yards away from them, rushing after him. By the end of the day, the students, exhausted and footsore, dragged themselves to their cars. Tucky looked just as he had at the start of the day, walking slowly and steadily.

After almost half a century of field work, Taliaferro had honed his technique so that age and infirmity were of little handicap. Naturally he had a tremendous advantage of experience over his followers—he could make and record observations more quickly—but there was more to it than that. He did two things that gave him the advantage over his students.

For one thing, he always knew where he was. By that I mean that he knew where his ground position was located on the map or aerial photograph that he was using as a base for geologic mapping. When he arrived at an outcrop, he already knew where it was on the base, because he had planned to go there from his last stop and would plan both on the map and on the ground where he would go next. The students spent a great deal of their time just trying to locate themselves on the base—in that case an airphoto. In the first place they were inexperienced at the technique, and in the second they didn't know in advance where Tucky had chosen to walk next. He was able to make his observations and leave an outcrop almost as soon as he got there. The students played catch-up all day.

The other thing Taliaferro did was to choose his next outcrop on the basis of what he wanted to learn about the geology of the area. In effect, he formulated a hypothesis about some aspects of the geology, made a prediction based on that hypothesis, chose an outcrop to test the prediction, and then went to look at it. If the prediction was verified, he retained the hypothesis and chose another outcrop to test it further. If the chosen outcrop did not verify the prediction, he would alter his hypothesis to account for the new bit of datum that didn't fit the old, now discarded, hypothesis, make a new prediction, and proceed to the next chosen outcrop.

The hapless students didn't function that way. They kept trying to locate themselves, and having done so, recorded data on their base map without much regard, if any, for how the data hung together and what it all meant in terms of the three-dimensional arrangement of the rocks beneath the surface. That task would be saved for later in tents, bars, or motel rooms when they had no opportunity to look at any more outcrops to test their interpretation. Lots of them would never get to be much better field geologists, but some would become skilled at the task, and those who excelled would do so because they learned to use some variant of Tucky's mode of operation.

I asked Tucky some years later if he did what I thought he did, and he just pulled at his mustache and slowly enunciated "G-o-o-o-d g-a-a-w-d no, Parker. I just go where I want to know something." Then he admitted that he supposed he did do the sort of thing I had surmised but that he'd never really thought about it. He just did it.

A geologic map is a record of a geologist's interpretation of the surface exposure of whatever rock types happen to underlie a given area. Generally, each rock type is assigned a map color or pattern so that the final map shows where any given rock type is located on the ground. The various rock symbols are separated by lines, called contacts, that indicate where one rock type gives way to another. Contacts may represent a place where one rock type was originally laid down over another, but that is a matter of interpretation.

Geologic maps also record information about the orientation of the rocks in space. For example, although most sedimentary rocks are initially deposited in more or less horizontal layers, earth processes generally tilt or bend them so that when observed in the field the layers are not horizontal. The geologist records the orientation of the layers on the map because that information is helpful in hypothesizing where the rocks are under the surface.

The geologic map is an interpretation and a simplification of the actual disposition of the rocks in the crust. In the first place, the bedrock is rarely totally exposed at the surface, although there are places such as the south coast of Norway where I did some field work where glacially smoothed surfaces are literally 100 percent exposed. In most places, the rocks are covered by soil, plants, broken rock debris, and water—not to mention highways, houses, and other works of man. The works of man are not entirely inimical to geologists' interests, because road cuts and other excavations frequently provide the best exposures in a region.

Most maps, then, are presented as continuous patterns or colors on the sheet of paper, but they result from a geologist visiting a limited number of outcrops and inferring what lies between them. In a general way, the more complete the exposure is, the closer the map is to reality, but even in superb exposure conditions the geologist cannot visit *every* outcrop and record *every* minor change in orientation of the rocks. Even the best map is a generalization of reality.

Because interpretation is such a significant factor in geologic mapping, field courses are usually offered at locations where exposure is far better than average so students can learn mapping where they have a lot of "facts" to deal with. (One result of this practice is that the western states are almost overrun with geology students, faculty, and staff during the summer. One suspects that beer sales in the mountain states must skyrocket when the field-course season arrives.) I put the word facts in quotes because at any given outcrop there may be differences in opinion among geologists. One may think that a given rock is the Dry Gulch Sandstone, whereas another thinks it has the characteristics of the East Overshoe Sandstone. A third imagines that it is neither of those, and so forth.

In addition to differences about the identity of a given outcrop, there is room for lots of arguments about the relations between adjacent mapped units. Is the contact a depositional one? Is it a fault contact? There is more than enough room for disagreement even among professional geologists. With students there can be really spectacular differences in interpretation, and grading maps of a field camp can be pretty entertaining—and sometimes depressing—when two student maps of the same place look as if they must have been produced in two different areas, and, worse yet, those areas apparently weren't the same ones the profs mapped either.

Differences between maps aren't always because of inexperience, either. I consider my old mentor Taliaferro to be a wonderful field geologist, but I would map some areas altogether differently than he did, and I would feel confident that I was right and he was wrong. He would have felt just the opposite. The difference is that he and I would map the rocks from a different perspective. He mapped highly deformed rocks in the Sierra Nevada foothills as if they were layers of sedimentary and volcanic rock thrown into horizontal wrinkles. I see the same rocks as rock units that bear little geometric relation to their precursor units, and I treat them as structural entities, mapping to determine their present arrangement in the crust without regard for some real or imagined primary stratigraphic arrangement. I view the structure as wrinkles that dive steeply into the crust.

Another factor in determining the closeness to reality of a geologic map is the scale of observation, and for a given area the scale of observation may depend on the amount of time spent to produce the map. A first stage in mapping a region is to do what is called reconnaissance mapping. That means driving around in a jeep, walking, flying over the area, using aerial photographs or satellite imagery, or any other technique that provides some broad generalities about the map area. When mapping layered sedimentary rocks, it is usual to try to find one or more places where the rock sequence can be observed in a presumably undisturbed state so that the normal character, sequence, and thicknesses of the units can be used as a standard. During a reconnaissance it is also usual to decide what map units to use, because the map cannot record every minuscule detail, so many times units are lumped together to form a map unit of convenient size. The field geologist chooses map units that are appropriate to the region under study. Layered rocks are often lumped into one or more units that are readily distinguished from one another, and are of suitable total thickness for the area in question. Often a highly distinctive unit may be chosen as a map unit even though it is quantitatively insignificant. For example, a thin limestone layer in a vast sequence of sandstones and shales might be just right for elucidating the structure of the whole region mapped, particularly if one layer of sandstone looked pretty much like any other layer.

After the reconnaissance the mapping begins, generally by a procedure that critics call chasing contacts. That means mapping the boundaries between units without looking within the units. Commonly, the contacts may be walked along and plotted, although it is also considered good form to locate the contacts at cross-cutting traverses and to connect them from one traverse to another. That procedure needn't be as sloppy as it sounds, because the trace of the contact is often clearly visible on an aerial photograph or can be sketched in on a map while sitting at one or more vantage points on the ground. In a well-exposed area, contact chasing will result in different geologists producing essentially identical maps that presumably must be "right."

However, contact chasing results in comparable maps only because the geologists have all agreed on the same ground rules at the beginning of the mapping. All have used the same arbitrarily defined units, and as long as they have correctly identified and located the boundaries between them, the maps almost have to agree. Even so, that agreement doesn't necessarily mean that the maps portray the real arrangement of the rocks.

Looking between the contacts may produce a great deal more information—in large part because of the additional detail gained by the mapper. As an example, I used to take the Wyoming field camp to a small anticlinal fold (an upward wrinkle) north of Vernal, Utah, for their first mapping experience. I discovered the place while flying over it in a light plane and chose it because it was almost totally exposed and was underlain by rock units that were easy to tell from one another—a perfect place for beginners.

The first year, both students and faculty chased contacts, and everyone's maps looked quite a bit alike. The next year, my teaching assistant Jim Sears, now a professor at the University of Montana, and I spent our time, in between helping students, looking at some details within the units on one flank of the fold. We found a complicated system of fault slices within two of the map units that thinned the units in some places and thickened and even repeated thin slivers of them in others—what a geologist calls structural complications. Those details were found simply by spending more effort in one small part of the map area. The next year, we spent our time on the top of the fold, which was dominated by one sandstone map unit. On careful study of the internal details of the one unit, we found we could recognize subunits. Mapping the subunits, we discovered that the crest of the "simple" anticline was itself a whole series of smaller folds that were shot through by numerous fault contacts. By increasing the number of map units, we had provided ourselves with a greater magnification of the rocks as it were. We didn't go back to that structure the next year, but if we had, we undoubtedly would have discovered still more complications. Our maps from one year to the next were as different as those from different geologists, yet it was more a matter of scale of observation and time available to look at finer and finer detail. On the scale of the geologic map of Utah, this complex bit of the crust is shown as a smooth bump on the end of a huge anticlinal fold that mostly lies within Dinosaur National Monument. In a general way, one could say that the more detailed the scale of observation, the more the final map represents reality.

In the real world, map areas are chosen almost by chance, rather than by designing geology professors who try to fit the difficulty of the mapping to the students' growing abilities. One takes what one gets and makes the most of it. In many areas, outcroppings are scattered through woods and open fields, with continuous exposures only in for-tuitous places such as road cuts, quarries, or stream bottoms. A geologist beginning to map in such a situation lacks the opportunity to get a broad view of the sweep of the rocks because even such generalities may be invisible from the ground or from above. Perhaps ridges may be underlain by resistant rocks and valleys by more easily eroded ones, but there may be few clues to the big picture to allow the field worker to formulate a working hypothesis, for that is the purpose of the reconnaissance. For the area near Vernal where Sears and I mapped I had a fairly complete, coarse scale initial hypothesis just from flying over it before I ever set foot on the place.

In a poorly exposed area, it may be more difficult to get that first hypothesis going. Let's assume that such an area is known, or assumed, to be underlain by a regular succession of sedimentary rocks whose character is known from some other location in the general vicinity. One would say that the regional stratigraphy was known. In that case, the geologist does have the initial hypothesis that the thickness and character of the rock units will be the same in the new area as in the other location. He can walk up to the first outcrop, examine it, and with luck conclude that he is dealing with the Smith Sandstone. Perhaps, though, the Smith Sandstone resembles the Horsehoe Sandstone, and he can't be sure which one he is dealing with. In that case he has to work with two hypotheses and test them both. In the geologic setting I've established, the test can be made on the basis of which units are stratigraphically below and above the first outcrop. Adjacent units can be examined and one hypothesis can be tentatively rejected. I say tentatively because the inital hypothesis based on knowing the regional stratigraphy includes an assumption that the rocks will be in a structurally undisturbed sequence. If faulting has taken place, then other alternatives are still possible, and further testing would need to be done at other outcrops.

Most geologists map with built-in prejudices that influence their testing of successive hypotheses. In the aforementioned example, a geologist whose experience was in relatively undisturbed terranes would favor the hypothesis that the rock units were in normal stratigraphic relationship to one another. Another mapper might have a background in regions where folding and faulting were widespread and might favor a structurally complex concept. Most geologists would apply Occam's Razor and make the initial assumption that normal, undisturbed stratigraphic relationships were preserved until evidence to the contrary was found. At that point, explanations from structural disturbance would be proposed and tested.

I have assumed to this point that the geologist does nothing but identify units and try to connect outcrops in such a way that contacts can be inferred and placed on the map. Most real mapping is then somewhat different from contact chasing in that actual contacts are seldom or never exposed and the mapper is really looking at the map area through sort of an opaque screen with little holes cut in various places. In its simplest form, such mapping is a bit like a laboratory exercise prepared by teachers in which units are identified as spots on a sheet of paper, perhaps with indications of the orientation of the layering, if any, and the students are asked to draw in contacts to make a geologic map.

In the field, an experienced geologist has a great deal more information available than that given to an unfortunate student in a lab section. The inclination of the boundaries between units can often be estimated in the field. In addition, there may be more information in the first outcrop than just rock type and orientation of layering. In sedimentary rocks there are commonly internal structural and textural features that indicate which direction is stratigraphically up or younger, sometimes called the direction of younging or the stratigraphic top. In this last example, if the geologist knew the direction of younging by examining the first outcrop he would know what unit to expect in that direction and could limit his choices.

Fossils are frequently found in sedimentary rocks and provide the geologist with more tools. William Smith, the English surveyor appropriately considered to be the father of geologic mapping, used fossils to demonstrate identity of units. An intriguing case of the use of fossils in mapping was reported in the journal *Geology* a short time ago. Geologists who were mapping a body of limestone in California sent samples to a paleontologist in Italy to see if she could determine the direction of younging of the mass from study of the microfossils in the unit. A short time later she wrote them to tell them the younging direction and also told them that there was a fault between two of their samples sites. They returned to the field, and sure enough, there was the fault that had been predicted from the vantage point of an Italian laboratory.

With a kit of tools that includes a stratigraphic succession, orientation of rocks in outcrop, sedimentary structures that determine top and bottom of layers, and fossils, the geologist has access to a variety of information.

The identity of bedrock can sometimes be inferred from the nature of overlying soils, provided that the soils weren't transported from elsewhere. In parts of the southeastern U.S. graphite-bearing rocks are mapped by rubbing soil between the hands. If a gray smudge remains, then the bedrock is supposed to be the graphitic unit. In Bordeaux the wines from grapes grown on chalk soils taste different from those grown on soils derived from other rocks, and a geologist with a discerning palate can map on that basis. (One does wonder how the organization footing the bill might view the geologist's expense account however.) Part of the mapping I did when I was a student at the Berkeley field camp was in a monotonous succession of alternating shales and sandstones. Taliaferro had learned that the soils formed from the two rocks were different and distinguished them by stamping his feet on them, since the shale soils feel springer than the sandstone ones.

Assembling a geologic map is not the ultimate goal of mapping. The map is an interpretation of the surface distribution of underlying bedrock and is just a way station toward a three-dimensional interpretation of how the rocks are disposed beneath the surface. Most geologists consider the subsurface configuration as the mapping progresses and judge the reasonableness of their map by how reasonable the third dimension required by the map is. Final maps are generally accompanied by so-called cross sections which are the mapper's view of how the various units would appear in one or more vertical slices through the subsurface. Cross sections are derived from the map and are really just maps of imaginary vertical planes through the earth.

Some mappers are able to make maps without thinking

about the subsurface. I had a student one summer who had not had a course in which she had been taught to construct cross sections. Her first ones were terrible, and we tried to help her, but the third dimension came hard to her. What was amazing was that her maps were excellent in all respects. She just didn't seem to have the faintest idea what was going on underground.

The cross section is a prediction that is often not testable, but in some instances wells or mine workings give some information at depth. In parts of the world where valuable underground mineral resources are exploited by wells or mines, the third dimension may be well known, and what amount to three-dimensional maps can be constructed.

The mapping that I have described so far is distinguished by the presence of that initial hypothesis of a regular stratigraphic succession of some sort made up of recognizable units with relatively consistent character and thickness. In many areas such regularity cannot be assumed. For example, the rocks may be changed in character by some geologic process. Solutions migrating through the rocks can alter their composition and appearance in many ways so that a rock unit no longer looks like the same unit in another part of the region. Limestones become replaced by silica, sandstones become bleached, shales baked red, and so forth. Such alteration of character can be discerned by careful work, however.

In the case of metamorphic rocks, there is a continuum from rocks that have undergone change but are still preserved in much their original character to sequences that bear little or no resemblance to the original rocks. The Precambrian Belt Series rocks in Montana are metamorphosed yet still bear abundant sedimentary structures and can be mapped using stratigraphic principles. Other metamorphic rocks have been folded repeatedly, recrystallized, ground up, partially melted, and lord knows what else. In such rocks, called tectonites because they owe much of their internal structure to earth movement or tectonism, layering may bear no relation to some original sedimentary layering but may have developed during the movements accompanying metamorphism.

Many geologists whose background and experience is with unmetamorphosed sedimentary rocks try to treat tectonites in the same way. They define map units, measure thicknesses of the units, establish a supposed stratigraphy, and start to map with that hypothesis as their basis. In most instances, their mapping project fails because they began with a false premise. Their conceptual view of mapping is to use stratigraphic relationships to produce a map and ultimately a three-dimensional inference of the geometry of the rock bodies. They try to use younging directions with rocks for which there is no such direction, for many metamorphic rocks are folded back on themselves over and over like a stack of accordion-pleated computer paper so that the original stratigraphic "up" may reverse itself every foot or inch or less just as the printed side of the paper reverses with every sheet.

How, then, does one map highly deformed and metamorphosed rocks? One does exactly as with ordinary sedimentary rocks except that no initial hypothesis is formulated about stratigraphic relationships. One might still do a reconnaissance study of the region to see what rock types are present and tentatively establish some mapping units, but no assumptions can be made about relations among the units in stratigraphic terms.

After a reconnaissance, the geologist visits the first outcrop. The outcrop will be composed of a given rock type, perhaps one of those provisionally designated as a map unit. Then the geologist will measure and record the orientation of the rock. At that point, the procedure takes on a completely different character, because most tectonites contain a great deal more information about their history than ordinary sedimentary rocks. To be sure they rarely contain fossils or indicators of the direction of younging, but they more than make up for that lack by the presence of a wealth of other features.

Tectonites are usually the result of multiple episodes of deformation and in an ideal case contain structural features that reflect each episode. An episode of deformation may produce a planar feature such as layering or a flattening of mineral grains that gives a platy aspect to the rock. On such surfaces there are also usually linear features. In addition, there are usually scattered small-scale folds that may be microscopic or on the scale of a large outcrop. In most tectonites there will be more than one system of such features.

Experience has shown that the small, outcrop-sized features are indicators of the larger-scale structure of the rocks. What the mapper of highly deformed rocks does is infer the large from the small. The geometric relationships shown in the outcrop provide the first hypothesis for the geometry of the whole.

With luck, the first outcrop will provide a great deal of information. In fact, if it doesn't, it is my practice to look around for an outcrop that does contain a lot of information, because then a working hypothesis can be formulated. In a suitable outcrop one is able to judge which features are the youngest in the sequence, because the latest episode of deformation not only leaves its own traces in the rock, but it also affects all previous minor features. Old planar structures may be folded or displaced by the new ones, old lineations may be bent, and older folds may be refolded around new directions. The time spent deciphering the relations in the first outcrop will pay off with a complicated hypothesis to test at subsequent outcrops. Such a hypothesis is almost a pure abstraction, because one is unable to trace any mappable units, yet one can make statements about the mutual relations among the discontinuous layers and other features.

The mapping proceeds much as with stratigraphic mapping except that there are more pieces of information to keep track of. The inferred relative age relations of the minor features may need revision, and old outcrops may have to be revisited to clear up ambiguities.

The mapper of tectonite terranes attempts to understand the structural geometry of the area in terms of the arrangement of a family of surfaces and linear features. When the geometry has been successfully worked out, it may be that some inferences about original stratigraphy emerge, but that is often not the case. The tectonite mapper has at once more information and less information than the mapper of less disturbed rocks. What earth processes take away by destruction of obvious stratigraphy is more than made up for by the wealth of new information added to the very fabric of the rock.

For me the mapping of tectonites provides the perfect happiness of the field geologist—an Elysian field as it were. The great fun about tectonites is that given the right initial outcrop, one can predict the whole outcome of a mapping project after an hour or so or even after just a few minutes in the field. With mapping based on a known stratigraphy, it is largely a matter of attention to detail and simply doing more work until the mapping makes sense. By contrast, tectonites allow for great leaps of the mind from the small to the great and from the present to the distant past. Tectonites are just plain fun to work with because they are so challenging.

I took one of my last graduate students at Wyoming, Bob Wells, to a potential field area, and we looked at one large outcrop that I had visited a year earlier. Bob was the kind of person who once drove clear from Laramie to Albuquerque just to hear Joni Mitchell. A person needs that sort of mixture of madness and devotion to understand tectonites. The outcrop that we looked at indicated that the layering originated from an ancient episode of folding, shearing, and stretching that transformed some unknown original rock into a new one which bore linear elements that were parallel to the hinges of old, now destroyed folded layers. I showed him how the old lineations in that outcrop were twisted around a later folding direction that had left its traces as occasional folds with their limbs parallel to one another. I hypothesized that the structure of the whole area would be just like that outcrop and that he'd find that the latest fold direction would be consistent throughout, and that he'd be able to follow the refolding of the first folds on a map scale, as well.

I wouldn't be relating this tale if he hadn't tested my idea and confirmed it as he did—brilliantly. After Bob's oral defense of his thesis, one member of the committee, a geologist turned geophysicist who, though he thought that he understood highly deformed rocks, was at heart a stratigraphic mapper, shook his head and said, "How in the world did he ever figure out that incredibly complicated structure with no stratigraphy and not even any mappable units?" I just smiled and said, "He's a smart kid." And he was.

Appendix

interval name	approximate duration, millions of years before present	% of total time	events, life forms
PHANEROZOIC TIME		12	
CENOZOIC ERA		1.4	
Quaternary Period			
Holocene Epoch	0.01–0.0	0.0002	modern man
Pleistocene Epoch	2.0–0.01	0.04	early man
Tertiary Period			
Pliocene Epoch	5.1–2.0	0.06	hominids
Miocene Epoch	24.6–5.1	0.41	Himalayan Mountains formed
Oligocene Epoch	38–24.6	0.28	
Eocene Epoch	54.9–38	0.35	early horses
Paleocene Epoch	65–54.9	0.21	early primates
MESOZOIC ERA		3.8	
Cretaceous Period	144–65	1.6	last of dinosaurs; Alps, Rockies formed

* Numerical values from Harland and others, 1982. Harland, W. B., A. C. Cox, P. G. Llewellyn, C. A. G. Pickton, A. G. Smith, and R. Walters, *A Geologic Time Scale.* (Cambridge: Cambridge University Press, 1982) .

GEOLOGIC TIME SCALE (*Continued*)

interval name	approximate duration, millions of years before present	% of total time	events, life forms
Jurassic Period	213–144	1.4	dinosaurs early birds, and mammals
Triassic Period	248–213	0.73	Atlantic Ocean formed
PALEOZOIC ERA		7.1	
Permian Period	286–248	0.79	reptiles
Carboniferous Period*	360–286	1.5	early reptiles, trees
Devonian Period	408–360	1.0	early trees
Silurian Period	438–408	0.62	early land plants
Ordovician Period	505–438	1.4	first fish
Cambrian Period	590–505	1.8	first shelled organisms
PRECAMBRIAN TIME		88	
PROTEROZOIC ERA	2,450–590	39	first complex organisms, oxygen in atmosphere
ARCHEAN ERA AND PRISCOAN ERA	4,800–2,450	49	bacteria and algae in last half of era

* Within the United States the Carboniferous Period is called the Carboniferous System and is subdivided into an older Mississippian Period and a younger Pennsylvanian Period.

Notes

CHAPTER ONE
The Buffer Did It

Coates, D. R., and J. D. Vitek. *Thresholds in Geomorphology*. London: Allen and Unwin, 1980.

Gilbert, G. K. *Report of the Geology of the Henry Mountains*. Washington, D.C.: U. S. Government Printing Office, 1877.

————. "The Transportation of Debris by Running Water." U. S. Geological Survey Professional Paper 86. Washington, D.C.: U. S. Government Printing Office, 1914.

Parker, Ronald B. *Inscrutable Earth*. New York: Charles Scribner's Sons, 1984 (especially Ch. 14).

————. "Buffers, Energy Storage, and the Mode and Tempo of Geologic Events." *Geology* 13 (1985): 440–442.

————. "Buffers, Energy Storage, and the Mode and

Tempo of Geologic Events—Reply." *Geology* 14 (1986): 265–266.

Schumm, S. A. "Buffers, Energy Storage, and the Mode and Tempo of Geologic Events—Discussion." *Geology* 14 (1986): 265.

CHAPTER TWO
The Urge to Surge

Kamb, Barclay, C. F. Raymond, W. D. Harrison, Hermann Engelhardt, K. A. Echelmeyer, N. Humphrey, M. M. Brugman, and T. Pfeffer. "Glacier Surge Mechanism: 1982–1983 Surge of Variegated Glacier, Alaska." *Science* 227 (1985): 469–479.

Kopf, Rudolph W. "Hydrotectonics: Principles and Relevance." U. S. Geological Survey Open File Report 82–307, 1982.

Paterson, W. S. B. *The Physics of Glaciers.* London: Pergamon, 1969.

CHAPTER THREE
From Order to Chaos and Back Again—a Case of Misunderstanding

Anon. "State of Controversy." *Scientific American* 254, no. 1 (1986): 62–63.

Buerger, M. J. *Elementary Crystallography.* New York: John Wiley and Sons, 1956.

Evans, R. C. *Crystal Chemistry.* London: Cambridge University Press, 1966.

Nelson, David R., and Betrand I. Halperin. "Pentagonal and Icosahedral Order in Rapidly Cooled Metals." *Science* 229 (1985): 233–238.

CHAPTER FOUR
Boron 93516

Barnard, Ralph M., and Robert B. Kistler. "Stratigraphic and Structural Evolution of the Kramer Sodium Borate Ore Body, Boron, California." *Symposium on Salt*. 2nd Cleveland 1965. Cleveland: Northern Ohio Geological Society, 1966.

Borchert, Hermann, and R. O. Muir. *Salt Deposits.* London: D. Van Nostrand, 1964.

Braitsch, O. *Salt Deposits: Their Origin and Composition.* New York: Springer Verlag.

Walker, C. T., ed. *Geochemistry of Boron.* Stroudsburg, PA: Dowdon, Hutchinson, and Ross, 1975.

CHAPTER FIVE
The Coral Clock and Other Lines of Evidence

Brenchley, P. J., ed. *Fossils and Climate.* New York: John Wiley and Sons, 1984.

Clark, George R., II. "Growth Lines in Invertebrate Skeletons." In *Annual Review of Earth and Planetary Sciences*, edited by F. A. Donath, F. G. Stehli, and G. W. Wetherill. Menlo Park, CA: Annual Reviews, Inc., 1974.

Jones, Douglas S. "Annual Cycle of Shell Growth Increment Formation in Two Continental Shelf Bivalves and its Paleoecologic Significance." *Paleobiology* 6 (1980): 331–340.

———. "Sclerochronology: Reading the Record of the Molluscan Shell." *American Scientist* 71 (1983): 384–391.

Voorhies, M. R. "Taphonomy and Population Dy-
namics of an Early Pliocene Vertebrate Fauna, Knox
County, Nebraska." *Contributions to Geology*, Special
Paper No. 1 (1969).

Wells, John W. "Coral Growth and Geochronometry."
Nature 197 (1963): 948–950.

CHAPTER SIX
Aqua Spectaculars and Other Disasters

Clague, J. J., and W. H. Mathews. "The Magnitude of
Jökulhlaups." *Journal of Glaciology*. 12 (1973): 501–
504.

Clarke, Garry K. C. "Glacier Outburst Floods from
"Hazard Lake," Yukon Territory, and the Problem of
Flood Magnitude Prediction." *Journal of Glaciology*
28 (1982): 3–21.

Malde, H. E. "The Catastrophic Late Pleistocene
Bonneville Flood in the Snake River Plain, Idaho."
U. S. Geological Survey Professional Paper 596.
Washington, D.C.: Government Printing Office, 1968.

Mathews, W. H. "Two Self-Dumping Ice-Dammed
Lakes in British Columbia." *Geographical Review*
55 (1965): 46–52.

Nye, J. F. "Water Flow in Glaciers: Jökulhlaups,
Tunnels, and Veins." *Journal of Glaciology* 17 (1976):
181–207.

Post, Austin, and Lawrence B. Mayo. "Glacier
Dammed Lakes and Outburst Floods in Alaska." U. S.
Geological Survey Hydrologic Atlas HA–455. Wash-
ington, D.C.: Government Printing Office, 1971.

Stone, Kirk H. "The Annual Emptying of Lake
George, Alaska." *Arctic* 16 (1963): 26–40.

Waitt, Richard B., Jr. "Case for Periodic, Colossal Jökulhlaups from Pleistocene Glacial Lake Missoula." *Geological Society of America Bulletin.* 96 (1985): 1271–1286.

CHAPTER SEVEN
Journey to the Center of the Earth

Bowen, N. L. *Evolution of the Igneous Rocks.* Princeton: Princeton University Press, 1928.

Ernst, W. G. *Petrologic Phase Equilibria.* San Francisco: W. H. Freeman, 1976.

Jayaraman, A. "The Diamond-Anvil High-Pressure Cell." *Scientific American.* 250, no. 4 (1984): 54–62.

Kozlovsky, Y. A. "The World's Deepest Well." *Scientific American.* 251, no. 6 (1985): 98–104.

Verne, Jules. *Journey to the Centre of the Earth.* London: Griffith and Farran, 1872.

CHAPTER EIGHT
Scat Song

Brönnimann, P. "Remarks on the Classification of Fossil Anomuran Coprolites." *Paläontologisches Zeitschrift* 46 (1972): 99–103.

Edwards, P. E., and Daniel Yatkola. "Coprolites of White River (Oligocene) Carnivorous Mammals: Origin and Paleoecologic and Sedimentologic Significance." *Contributions to Geology* 13 (1974): 67–73.

Hansen, R. M. "Shasta Ground Sloth Food Habits, Rampart Cave, Arizona." *Paleobiology* 4 (1978): 302–319.

Hantzschel, Walter, F. El-Baz, and G. C. Amstutz.

Coprolites: An Annotated Bibliography, Geological Society of America Memoir 108, 1968.

Fry, G. F., and J. G. Moore. *"Enterobius vermicularis:* 10,000-Year-Old Human Infection." *Science* 166 (1969): 1620.

Mannheim, B. R. S. "A New Conception of the Formation of the Kola Peninsula Apatite Deposit: The Coprogenic Impact Theory—CIT." *Journal of Irreproducible Results* 25, no. 1 (1979): 6–7.

Moore, J. G., B. K. Krotoszynski, and H. J. O'Neill. "Fecal Odorgrams: A Method for Partial Reconstruction of Ancient and Modern Diets." *Digestive Diseases and Sciences* 29 (1984): 907–911.

Schäfer, Wilhelem. *Ecology and Palaeoecology of Marine Environments.* Translated by I. Oertel. Chicago: University of Chicago Press, 1972.

Whitehouse, F. W. "A Large Spiral Structure from the Cretaceous Beds of Western Queensland." *Memoirs of the Queensland Museum* 10 (1934): 203–211.

CHAPTER NINE
When Vulcan Speaks

Christiansen, R. L. "Yellowstone Magmatic Evolution: Its Bearing on Understanding Large Volume Explosive Volcanism." In *Explosive Volcanism: Inception, Evolution, and Hazards,* National Research Council Geophysics Study Committee. Washington, D.C.: National Academy Press, 1984.

Lambert, M. B. *Volcanoes.* Seattle: University of Washington Press, 1978.

Macdonald, G. A. *Volcanoes.* Englewood Cliffs, NJ: Prentice Hall, 1972.

Stothers, R. B. "The Great Tambora Eruption in 1815 and Its Aftermath." *Science* 224 (1984): 1191–1198.

Williams, Howel, and A. R. McBirney. *Volcanology.* San Francisco, Freeman, Cooper, and Co., 1979.

CHAPTER TEN
The View from Olympus

Goetz, A. F. H., G. Vane, J. E. Solomon, and B. N. Rock. "Imaging Spectrometry for Earth Remote Sensing." *Science* 228 (1985): 1147–1153.

Kahle, A. B., and A. F. H. Goetz. "Mineralogic Information from a New Airborne Thermal Infrared Multispectral Scanner." *Science* 222 (1983): 24–27.

Parker, R. B., ed. *ERTS Issue: Contributions to Geology* 12 (1973).

Sainsbury, C. L., K. J. Curry, and J. C. Hamilton. *An Integrated System of Geologic Mapping and Geochemical Sampling by Light Aircraft.* U. S. Geological Survey Bulletin 1361. Washington, D.C.: Government Printing Office, 1973.

Siegal, B S., and J. R. Gillespie. *Remote Sensing in Geology.* New York: John Wiley and Sons, 1980.

CHAPTER ELEVEN
Salt Rising

Gussow, W. C. "Salt Temperature: A Fundamental Factor in Salt Dome Intrusion." *Nature* 210 (1966): 518–519.

Kent, P. E. "Temperature Conditions of Salt Dome Intrusions." *Nature* 211 (1966): 1387.

Odé, Helmer. "Review of Mechanical Properties of

Salt Relating to Salt Dome Genesis." Geological Society of America Special Paper 88, 1968.

Talbot, C. J. "Halokinesis and Thermal Convection." *Nature* 273 (1980): 739–741.

Talbot, C. J., and R. J. Jarvis. "Age, Budget and Dynamics of an Active Salt Intrusion in Iran." *Journal of Structural Geology* 6 (1984): 521–533.

Talbot, C. J., and E. A. Rogers. "Seasonal Salt Movements in a Salt Glacier in Iran." *Science* 208 (1980): 395–397.

CHAPTER TWELVE
The .07 Percent Solution

Bögli, A. "Kalkosung und Karrenbilding." *Zeitschrift fur Geomorphologie* 2 (1960): 4–21.

————. "Erosion par Melange des Eaux." *International Journal of Speleology* 1 (1964): 61–70.

Cvijić, J. "Das Karstphanomen." *Geographisches Abhandlungen* 5 (1893): 225–275.

Ritter, D. F. *Process Geomorphology.* Dubuque, Iowa: William C. Brown, 1978.

Sanders, E. M. "The Cycle of Erosion in a Karst Region (after Cvijic)." *Geographical Review* 11 (1921): 593–604.

Sweeting, M. M. *Karst Landforms.* New York: Columbia University Press, 1973.

————. "The Karst of Kweilin. Southern China." *Geographical Journal* 144 (1978): 199–204.

Thrailkill, J. "Chemical and Hydrologic Factors in the Excavation of Limestone Caves. "*Geological Society of America Bulletin* 79 (1968): 19–46.

————. "Carbonate Chemistry of Aquifer and Stream Water in Kentucky." *Journal of Hydrology*. 16 (1972): 93–104.

Wood, W. W. "Origin of Caves and other Solution Openings in the Unsaturated (Vadose) Zone of Carbonate Rocks: A Model for CO_2 Generation." *Geology* 13 (1985): 822–824.

CHAPTER THIRTEEN
Where the Buffalo Roam

Haynes, C. V. "Were Clovis Progenitors in Beringia?" In *Paleoecology of Beringia*, edited by Hopkins, D. M., J. V. Matthews, Jr., C. E. Schweger, and S. B. Young. New York: Academic Press, 1982.

Markgraf, Vera. "Late Pleistocene Faunal Extinctions in Southern Patagonia." *Science* 228 (1985): 1110–1112.

Martin, P. S., and R. G. Klein, eds. *Quaternary Extinctions*. Tucson: University of Arizona Press, 1984.

Martin, P. S., and H. E. Wright, Jr. *Pleistocene Extinctions: The Search for a Cause*. New Haven: Yale University Press, 1967.

Nitecki, M. H. *Extinctions*, Chicago: University of Chicago Press, 1984.

Van Valen, L. "Late Pleistocene Extinctions." *Proceedings of the North American Paleontological Convention* 1 (1969): 469–485.

CHAPTER FOURTEEN
Elysian Fields

Chamberlin, T. C. "The Method of Multiple Working Hypotheses." *Journal of Geology* 5 (1897): 837–848.

Compton, R. R. *Manual of Field Geology.* New York: John Wiley and Sons, 1962.

Gilbert, G. K. "The Inculcation of Scientific Method by Example, with an Illustration Drawn from the Quaternary Period of Utah." *American Journal of Science* 31 (1886): 284–299.

Moseley, F. *Methods in Field Geology.* San Francisco: W. H. Freeman, 1981.

Index

Pauling, Linus, 44
Petroleum deposits, with salt
   domes, 140
petrology, experimental, 88
pillows, salt, 143, 148
pixel, 129
planar and linear structures, 197
plant communities, change of with
   climate, 175
plateau basalts, 114
Pleistocene extinction, 169–81
pollen studies, 171, 174
point groups, 39, 41
Pocatello, Idaho, 73
Post, Austin, 28, 29
potential energy, 32
prediction, 77, 118, 186
pressures, examples of, 89
Preston, Idaho, 73
pronghorn, 174, 176, 179
Pumpelly, Raphael, 138

Q

quartz crystals, form of, 35

R

radar imagery, 131
radiometric dating, 63, 168
Rampart Cave, Nevada, 103
Rang el Melah, Algeria, 139
Raymond, C. F., 29–30
reconnaissance mapping, 189, 196
Red Rock Pass, Idaho, 73
remote sensing, 125–36
Rigby, Keith, Jr., 20
ripple marks, giant, 80
road cuts, benefits of, 187, 191
rock deformation, 93–94, 196–197
rodents, diversity of, 169
Rogers, Eric, 146
Romer, Al, 110
rotation of the earth, 63
ruminants, advantages of, 176

S

salt
   anticlines, 143
   buoyant rising of, 139, 143
   diapir mechanism, 139
   domes, 138–48
   glaciers, 139, 146
   mines, 137, 138
   pillows, 143, 148
sampling, aerial, low technology,
   134
Santorin volcano, 123
satellite imagery, 128–30
scablands, 78
scat, 96–110
Schumm, Stan, 10
sea waves. *See* tsunamis
Searles Lake, California, 52–54
Sears, Jim, 190–91
seawater in sedimentary rocks, 50
sedimentation, cyclic, 11
seismic discontinuities, 87
seismology, 86, 118
shale, weathering of, 51
Shaw, E. W., 140
Shechtman, Daniel, 40–44
shell layers, origin of, 105
shorelines, ancient, 79
Siberia, 137, 178
silicon-oxygen linkage in lavas, 115
sinkholes, 151–52, 154, 162
Skylab photography, 130
Smith, William, 193
Snake River, 73
sodium carbonate lakes, 49, 51
sodium chloride, 49–50, 137, 141
soil, 156–57, 194
space groups, 36–37, 39, 41–44
speleologist, 153
stalactites and stalagmites, 152–53,
   160–61
Stassfurt, Germany, 49
Steensen, Niels, 35